# POINT B

## A Short Guide to
## Leading a Big Change

### by Peter Bregman

SPACE
FOR CHANGE

Space For Change, New York, 2007

Cover and Interior Design by Kristin Mulzer
Illustrations by Alison Stephen and Kristin Mulzer

ISBN-13: 978-0-9793872-0-3
ISBN-10: 0-9793872-0-5

Printed in the United States

*To Dr. Allan Rosenfield,*

*Thank you for your friendship, your integrity,
your caring, and your vulnerability. You are a role
model for all of us who believe that one person
can change the world.*

Acknowledgements:

First and foremost I want to thank my clients, without whom I would never have written a single word. Thank you for your trust, your collaboration, and your willingness to experiment with me. Working with you is a privilege that I do not take for granted; I am deeply grateful.

Thank you to the amazing team of Bregman Partners Associates – the creativity, diligence, and depth of experience you generously contribute to our work together appears all over these pages. I want to especially thank Andy Geller and Beth Fletcher, two of my cherished mentors who are extraordinary consultants and whose fingerprints appear in my work to this day.

Thank you Howie Jacobson for your wisdom and your generosity as a friend and partner. You continue to be an inspiring collaborator – brilliant and human, thoughtful and funny.

A special thanks to Paul Burger and Michael Schell for your advice, interest, and unrelenting support. Thank you Kristin Mulzer for your creativity and skill. You made a tremendous difference to this book.

Thank you Mama and Papa for always believing in me. Thank you Anthony and Bertie for making fun of me when I take myself too seriously and encouraging me when I don't take myself seriously enough.

Most deeply, thank you Eleanor, Isabelle, Sophia and Daniel for your love, wisdom, friendship and presence in my life.

# CONTENTS

INTRODUCTION .............................................1

## PART 1: ALL ABOARD

A Journey Of Change .....................................9
The Three Attributes Of People Who Change.............19
The Engagement Continuum.....................................27

## PART 2: CREATING CHANGE

Strategy 1: Share The Story .........................................49
Strategy 2: Keep Everything Simple ........................67
Strategy 3: Get It Half Right ......................................81
Strategy 4: Integrate The Change................................95
Strategy 5: Provide Ongoing Support.......................113
Strategy 6: Build In Feedback ..................................131
Strategy 7: Use The Partner System .........................143

CONCLUSION ..................................................153

# Introduction

Long before I had any inkling that I would one day run a company specializing in organizational change, I learned an unexpected, hands-on, life lesson in change management. My first job out of college was with Outward Bound, an outdoor adventure school that teaches character skills such as leadership, teamwork, trust-building, and risk-taking. I had been working for about a year as a Course Director with Outward Bound focusing on corporate clients when my manager called me into his office and asked me to lead a 2-day retreat for 150 participants..

"Great," I thought, "that's larger than we've done so far – I'm glad I was chosen to lead it."

"Are they all from the same organization?" I asked. "Yep," he answered as he passed me the paperwork. He smiled a strange sort of smile – a smile I was only later able to interpret as slightly sadistic.

I went back to my desk, filled up a hot mug of tea, and sat down to read the details of this retreat. I read the first page, burned my tongue, and shot back to his office. "You gave me the wrong paperwork," I told him.

"No mistake," he said, "You'll do fine. You might even learn something." I went back to my desk and reviewed the background. They <u>were</u> all from the same organization: a Junior High School in New Jersey. I was responsible for a group of 150 eighth graders for a weekend.

"Well," I thought, "this is a challenge – and who better to do it than me? I was once an eighth grader."

I planned the way I usually did and a week before the course I brought eight instructors into a room for a full-day meeting. In front of each instructor was a clean, well organized folder including the names of the kids in each small group, a schedule of the activities, grocery lists, where they were supposed to be and when. I had planned everything. I was the leader, they were my followers. We spent a long day going over the details. I wasn't leaving anything to chance. Some of the instructors complained that they felt constrained; that there was too much planned; that this activity or that activity wouldn't work. I listened to them and responded that I recognized it would be hard but that I had my full trust in their capability: they were the best instructors at Outward Bound and that was why I asked them to be on this retreat – I knew they could make it work. I felt pretty good about my leadership. I was doing everything right. Just like I read in the 20 leadership books on my bookshelf.

We stood outside the retreat center a week later when four Greyhound buses came barreling through the entrance gate, a cloud of dust following behind. The minute the first kid stepped off the bus it was chaos.

No one listened. Not during my welcome speech, not while we split them into groups, not for bagels and orange juice. And it only got worse. Two kids got into a fight, another fell and was bleeding, and worst of all, they were bored and made no secret of it. "I'm bored." "This sucks." I was getting the clue. And yet, I didn't have a clue. I was terrified. I didn't know what to do. I was in over my head and my planning hadn't saved me. I was distraught. I was failing. But worse – the failure wasn't complete yet – we were only half a day into a two-day program. I had much further to fall.

I panicked. I thought through all of my options. I came up with nothing which terrified me even more. I didn't know what to do next. I didn't have the answer.

I left the office, asked the teachers to manage lunch, and called all the instructors together for a meeting. I was raw, scared, and feeling helpless. "I have failed you. This is going terribly and I have no idea how to turn it around. To be honest with you, I have no idea what to do."

There was an awkward silence as the instructors looked at me, watching the person who was always in control lose it and reach out to them for help. Then one woman with whom I had several disagreements in the past started to speak. "Here it comes," I thought, "she's gonna make me suffer." She smiled and told me that she had a background in theater and would love to collect the kids who wanted to participate and do some improvisational theater about issues they were facing as new teenagers. "And perhaps they could then perform for the whole group as an after-dinner activity," she added. Another instructor spoke up: "There's a great hike to the fire tower over the hill. I could take some kids up there with the Polaroids and do some cool instant photography."

One by one each of the instructors came up with an idea that drew on their strengths and would create a great experience for the kids. As I was listening, I felt deeply touched. They were pulling through. They had critical competencies that I didn't even know about; that I had not bothered to discover. And most of all, they were generous with their support and talents.

One of the biggest surprises came when these instructors gave me feedback. I received the highest scores on my leadership that I had ever received. And this became one of the most innovative retreats that Outward Bound had executed. It completely redefined the meaning of leadership for me. It wasn't my responsibility to have all the answers. On the contrary, *it was my responsibility to know that I did not have all the answers.* People were much higher performers when they could be relied on to make choices themselves. When they were engaged in the process. When they had choice and control. The hard part was that for them to have control, I had to give up control.

In that experience, I learned that change was an opportunity. It is sometimes hard to imagine this because change is also a breakdown. Most change occurs when something is no longer working. Profits are down, sales are down, people are leaving, the strategy isn't being implemented, managers and employees aren't talking to each other, customers aren't being served, morale is low.

That's also the opportunity of change – to move people from point A to point B – to realign the organization behind its most important objectives, to unleash the workforce in pursuit of those objectives, and to support them when they need it. People can then see where they can make an impact. How to shift from a whiner to an actor. Given the right support, everyone can be in a position to own a change. Each person can be put into the position where they are responsible for critical strategic decisions and actions. In such an organization, people feel important, needed, and valued *because they are.*

On my team, like in many corporations, people felt undervalued, under utilized, and ignored. Unfortunately, most change efforts reinforce those feelings. But they don't have to. Everyone can and should feel valued and respected. This is not just touchy-feely sentiment. It is the difference between an organization that succeeds and one that fails. Change is an opportunity to send the message that every person matters. That it takes the efforts, talents, advice, and decisions of each person to get to point B.

People make and face life changes everyday. They move, get married, start families, face challenges, learn new technologies, change jobs and develop new skills. Not all of these changes occur without some resistance, not all are easy and entirely smooth. However, most of the time, given life changes or obstacles, human beings show remarkable resiliency, and are generally successful at adapting well to new situations. It is startling to know, then, that 70% of all corporate change efforts fail.

Why are people more apt to be resilient and adaptive throughout changing personal lives, yet resistant to change as members of organizations?

When change is successful it is because everyone involved in the change feels ownership for its success. Resistance is a by-product of the way we try to change people, of flawed strategies for getting "buy-in." People resist being controlled. Trying to sell, motivate or coerce members of an organization devalues them. This book is a guide to help you lead change without resistance. In Part One, I explain what it means to own change and I describe the conditions necessary for people to own change. In Part Two, I offer seven strategies for creating those conditions. These strategies are the key to moving people from point A to point B.

> PEOPLE DON'T RESIST CHANGE, THEY RESIST BEING CHANGED.

# Part 1:
# ALL ABOARD

# A Journey of Change

I still remember the excitement of winning the contract – I called one of Bregman Partners' advisors from the street as soon as I heard: "We got it! We're running the change effort for 2000 people globally!" He was silent for a moment and then spoke gravely, "Don't be so proud of yourself. It's one thing to win the contract. Another to make it a success."

"Hmm." I thought, "What's his problem?"

The next day I joined the small group of change leaders who were struggling with a 250-person pilot that was not going well. People were not complying. Having learned from my Outward Bound experience – or so I thought – I asked the leaders to shift their perception of pilot participants. To think of them as leaders too, not just a "compliance problem." Instead of selling pilot participants on the change, we should ask for their help. It was, after all, a pilot. They agreed.

We spoke with all pilot participants. We told them that

we were committed to change but did not know the best way to run the program and needed their advice and involvement. What would help them most? What worked and what didn't? What problems came up and how should we solve them? We were candid with participants: we were learning with them and we needed their guidance. We listened to them. They began to take responsibility for the change. They began to own their change. The pilot became a great success.

Then, with all the knowledge gained from the pilot we, the small group of leaders who ran the pilot, began to design the full rollout. This change involved thousands of people and the logistics were complicated. Concerned about turnover and customer complaints in its Technology division, the firm wanted to improve communication and employee development for 2,000 people across three continents. At the time, fewer than 50% of employees were receiving performance reviews. They were heard complaining, "It's easier to talk to a headhunter about my career than it is to talk to my manager."

The leaders had already redesigned the performance review and attempted several training programs to increase communication between managers and employees. This signified a major change for employees and managers alike. Suddenly, everyone was told to have very difficult conversations about performance using strange new language. They would all be measured against a new set of criteria.

Resistance was already high. People were simultaneously unclear what was expected of them and convinced they would not have the time to do it. Turnover was at its height at over 13%. This change meant a significant amount of work beyond their "real" work, which was already keeping them at the office 12 hours a day. "This is the third program like this in three years," we heard, "It'll pass." Confused, managers were justifiably concerned they would look inept in front of their employees.

After debriefing the pilot, we spent several weeks working out the details of the change plan. Without realizing it at the time, our perception began to shift. This was no longer a pilot; it was the real thing, with little room for error. We morphed back into an exclusive group of leaders defining the change for everyone else. We were going to figure out the *perfect* design to pull it off! This thought alone should have been our first warning that we were headed for disaster.

We plowed through different designs, planning how to define roles, set up reporting, send out communications, divide thousands of people into manageable groups and create a schedule. We tried to think of everything. We split the thousands into "classes" of 100, each led by a pair of consultants who would guide people through the change. We carefully spread out the launch so that a new class would start every few weeks, thereby controlling the crunch periods. The final design was a 40 page document, color-coded by class and start date. It was pretty. That should have been our second (big fat) warning.

PRETTY
DELIVERABLES
DELAY CHANGE

This project involved over 30 Bregman Partners consultants, trainers, and coaches. We held a kick-off meeting for the consultants, describing the plan and answering questions effectively. We had prepared lots of documents – frequently asked questions (FAQs), calendars, training scripts, trouble shooting sheets, Power Point presentations – and placed them all in fully packed, neat binders. All consultants' roles were clearly defined. They knew what to do and how to do it. I was the leader of the group and the project manager – they should see me about any problems and I would resolve them. I was in control. That should have been my third warning.

CENTRALIZED CONTROL BLOCKS OWNERSHIP

We launched the program and the first month went smoothly. We sent out the right emails at the right time and the first few "classes" went without a hitch. Treating participants as change targets, we told them how the process would work, what was expected of them over the course of the year-long program rollout, and why it was a good thing. I held hour-long weekly meetings with all consultants to ensure I was on top of any problems. I remember thinking to myself, once again, "This is a great design – it's really going smoothly." Two months into the program, I was on top of all the details. I knew just about everything that was happening in the program. That should have been our fourth warning.

IF YOU ARE ON
TOP OF ALL THE
DETAILS, THEN
THERE AREN'T
ENOUGH DETAILS

Then the problems began to crop up. People started to complain that the program was not meeting their needs: it would take too much time and they were not sufficiently prepared. They had questions about the process that went beyond the knowledge of some of the consultants (I knew the answers – it was my design, after all; but I wasn't teaching all the classes). At times, in an effort to maintain control and leadership, the consultants made fair and educated guesses as to the answers. Some of those answers were wrong, and rumors started to fly about problems with the program. Some consultants were singled out as incompetent. Some of the consultant pairs began to lose confidence in each other's capabilities.

And of course – everyone was coming to me with these problems. And they were right to come to me. After all, I was the person who was supposed to be in control. The super leader. So I tried to play my role as super leader; I problem solved, I calmed people down, I wrote more FAQs, I sent out emails of things never to say or do in front of clients, I set up a bulletin board system so that we could post lessons learned. I slept about 3 hours a night.

Remember our pretty design? New classes starting every few weeks? Well, with each new class came a whole set of new problems, new mistakes, and new "issues" that threatened the program. The first month, 200 people were in the program. Two weeks later, it was 400. Two weeks after that, it was 600.

It was speeding out of control. I tried to manage the program more closely, thinking that if only I had been more involved, these problems would not have happened. I lengthened the hour-long weekly meetings to two hours and started holding conference calls between meetings to troubleshoot more immediate problems. Four consultants had to leave the program and several others were struggling. Participants were beginning to lose confidence.

I remember one night being driven home in a company car at 2 am feeling like I was in the biggest mess of my life and not knowing how to get myself out of it. I was confused, sad, and lost.

I had two distinct and conflicting thoughts. One: I should quit and give this up – who am I fooling thinking that I could run this program? Two: I am learning something that I need to learn very badly (even though I didn't know what it was yet) and if I give up now, I will miss an important opportunity and lesson. And lose an important (and profitable) client.

I felt like I was swimming underwater in a large muddy lake and I couldn't see far enough ahead to know where I was going. I had to move forward, feeling my way, without knowing for sure that I was even moving in the right direction. I could only hope.

What had gone wrong? Why was this so out of control? The pilot worked so well! Why wasn't it translating into a successful program? I began to look at the difference between the pilot and the full rollout. In the pilot we didn't know the answers – we treated participants as co-leaders – we asked them to join us, help us, provide input and direction. *It was their program and we wanted to know what would work for them.* In the full rollout, we treated participants as change targets, as people who needed to comply with our plans. We had the answers. We told them how it would work. We didn't ask for their input because we had already gotten it from their colleagues and we had no more questions. We were the experts; the leaders. They were the targets of our expertise; the compliers.

I remembered what my advisor said to me when I first told him I won the project: "Don't be so proud of yourself." I also remembered my experience leading the retreat for eighth graders so long ago with Outward Bound: I was my own biggest obstacle.

As the architects of the change, we thought of ourselves as the *only* leaders, and tried to control everything. We gave all consultants the same role and the same plan, regardless of their skills and expertise. We took participants from different business units, with varying needs, and put them in the same class, giving them the same information, rules, and processes. We resisted their resistance. "The plan is strong," we thought, "People just aren't getting it."

I realized that, as initial leaders, we were making our job much harder than it needed to be. We were taking responsibility for the learning and accomplishments of the entire organization; acting as though it were our job to convince everyone to change. Our ownership was blocking everyone else from taking ownership..

The only hope of success for this change would be to run the whole effort like a pilot. To transfer leadership power to the consultants and participants. I split the consultants into five teams, each responsible for a business unit. These consultant teams were charged with going to the business units to find out what they wanted and what would work best for them. How were they currently communicating, what was the problem, and how would they like to see it solved? What did they need to learn? What worked for them?

The consultants knew the objectives of the program. They also knew they could be flexible to achieve those objectives to meet the needs of their clients. They didn't bring every problem to me for resolution; instead they went to the business units and asked them to resolve their own problems. They facilitated the process – but the business units owned it. We did not do focus groups with business units and then apply that knowledge to the rest of the program. This WAS the program. Everyone was more engaged. They were all leaders, in control of their own change.

This also decentralized the change. By moving control to the business units, our effort morphed from a program to an integrated change. Each business unit approached it differently – and all achieved their objectives. Each consultant approached it differently – and all were successful. Decentralizing the rollout was critical to its success.

I am often asked about consistency. Isn't it important to ensure that the organization as a whole is adhering to the program consistently? How else can you measure its success? How else will you know if people are really doing it? Don't you need to establish some order? Otherwise people could do anything, or worse, nothing!

CONSISTENCY IS ONLY
IMPORTANT IF IT
HELPS ACHIEVE
YOUR OBJECTIVES.

In this case, the objective was for employees and managers to have meaningful conversations. Everything else – performance review forms, the standards in the forms, trainings – was in the service of that objective. It is very possible for people to go through all the right motions and miss the objective. Better to be inconsistent in the tools and processes (give that control to others) and achieve the objective, offering support when it is needed or requested.

During this change effort, 2000 change targets transformed into 2000 change leaders. They were given choices in how to achieve their objectives and they made those choices. In the end, turnover decreased from 13% to 3%. Performance review completion went from 50% to 95%. The culture has changed; the division is engaged in an ongoing and energetic conversation about management skills, and business units went from tolerating to requesting to demanding a learning and development program in management. And as I write this, nine years later, these results have been sustained. The change has stuck because everyone in the organization owns it and chooses to maintain it.

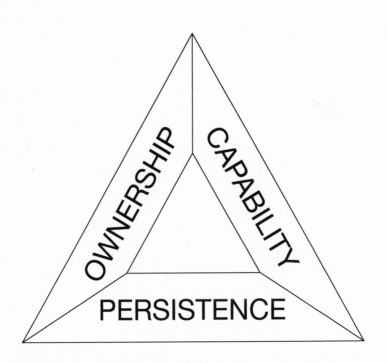

# The Three Attributes of People Who Change

There are three attributes that distinguish people who resist a change from people who embrace a change. A person who has all three attributes has the potential to be a change leader, enabling them to drive the change. If one attribute is missing, change will fail. If change is failing, the attributes can be used as a diagnostic. Help people acquire the missing attribute(s) and they will embrace or lead the change.

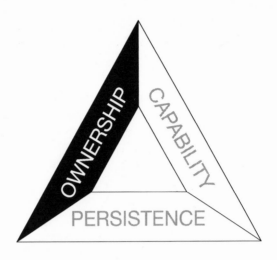

## Ownership

Change leaders *own* change. Ownership is the desire and commitment to make something happen. It is about having a stake in the outcome because *I* feel responsible for it – because *I* care about the result. It is not hard to create the conditions for ownership. People need one thing: a voice.

At a talk I gave recently, someone in the audience described a situation to underscore this point. The head of his division wanted him to move to a different job. The man was hesitant; he was successful in his current job and not inclined to move. The head of the division pushed: he described all the benefits, told him it was a good career move, and offered extra money. The man finally agreed. Two months later, unhappy, he asked to go back to his old job. "You're doing fine," the head of his division told him, "You'll eventually settle in to it. Give it more time." Four months later the man left the company and the head of the division lost a loyal, hard working employee and a substantial amount of intellectual capital. I asked him why he left. "The head of the division never asked me what I wanted. He told me what I wanted. At first, I bought it. But after a while, I realized I wanted something different."

Most leaders are very persuasive. Their ability to influence is one of the skills that got them to the position of leadership in the first place. But persuasiveness backfires when used to convince others to do things they don't want to do. It creates resistance – often quiet, pernicious resistance.

PEOPLE "OWN" WHAT THEY CONTROL.

Giving people some control encourages resilience. On the other hand, trying to control or coerce them leads to resistance, which is their way of regaining control.

The hardest part for you if you are trying to get someone to change? Letting go of control. Letting go of the need to force compliance and allowing people to make decisions for themselves.

Following the 7 Change Strategies outlined in Part 2 of this book ensures that while you let go of control, your change effort does not spin out of control.

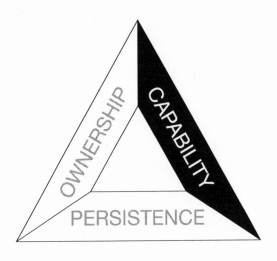

## Capability

Simply stated, if you *can't* do something, you *won't* do it, at least not successfully. Capability involves knowing and doing; both acquiring information and applying it. People who change successfully focus on a small amount of information and apply it successfully.

If I am implementing a strategy to move my business onto the Internet, I need to know how to create value in electronic form, and how to market that value. That's the *acquisition* of information. Unfortunately most change efforts stop there.
More than information, I need the skill to translate a concept into action. I might know everything about creating value on the Internet, but does that mean I can actually do it? I can read all about a great tennis serve. Does that mean I can actually hit one? People who change develop true capability by trying, failing, reflecting, and trying again.

Most change efforts attempt to create capability through

training and communications. But few people are impacted by these methods. Studies show that 90% of people do *nothing differently* six months after training. That's because capability doesn't grow in a classroom or a newsletter; it grows on the job. While you work. While you speak with colleagues. While you troubleshoot a particularly difficult problem. While you negotiate. Actually, training programs can retard your capability because they take time away from your learning.

There are three stages to developing true capability:

1. **Awareness**
   Discovering one's own strengths and weaknesses, learning new skills, and increasing one's knowledge and understanding of new ways to act.

2. **Accountability**
   Understanding the implications for taking action based on the new awareness, and creating plans to take targeted actions. Becoming personally responsible for taking new actions and seeing the results that follow.

3. **Action**
   Actually taking the actions, learning from feedback, and demonstrating the behaviors that will get the desired results.

Training and communications create awareness but do not generate accountability or action, the two essential levers of behavior change. That's why during most change efforts, people remain unchanged – more aware but no more capable. In contrast, successful change efforts support people as they take accountability for, and action with, new skills.

**Persistence**

This is the most challenging of the three attributes, and is often overlooked.

The desire to change may be strong for a moment. But the success of change happens over time. I may have the ownership and capability to make a change but if I do not persist in my practice, I will ultimately fail. People who successfully implement change take small daily actions on an ongoing basis. They have the resources to follow through on their decisions, the commitment to stay focused on making the change happen, the willingness to be a role model, and the courage to prioritize the change over time.

When you learn something new you will be out of your comfort zone and you will experience some failure. With persistence, failure is an opportunity to develop, to actually increase your capability and ownership. Without persistence, failure simply becomes a good excuse not to try again.

## The Three Attributes of People Who Change

For change to succeed, the three attributes of people who change must be cultivated in all people so they become successful in their change. The way to do that is by seeing all people as change leaders in the first place and deeply engaging them in every aspect of the change effort.

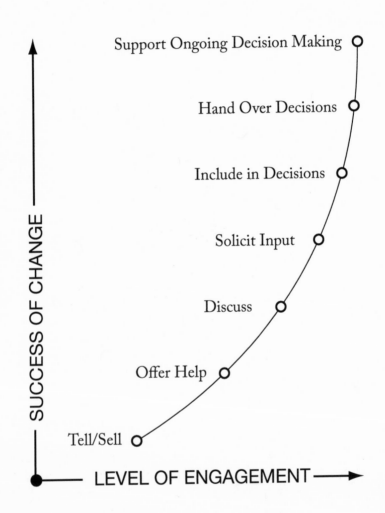

Support Ongoing Decision Making

Hand Over Decisions

Include in Decisions

Solicit Input

Discuss

Offer Help

Tell/Sell

SUCCESS OF CHANGE

LEVEL OF ENGAGEMENT ⟶

# The Engagement Continuum

The Engagement Continuum correlates various activities with their success rates in helping people and organizations change. The Continuum illustrates that the more we engage people around the change we're asking them to make, the more likely they are to own it and develop their capability. And the more consistently we support them along the way, the more likely they will take the many small acts of courage necessary to go from beginner to master. If they own it, develop their capability, and persist, they will change.

Nothing is wrong with activities at the lower levels of the Continuum; they are critical pieces of any change program. The problem arises when a change effort consists exclusively of these lower-level activities. The higher-level activities are the glue that ensures a change will stick. At these higher levels, everyone in the organization takes personal responsibility for making change succeed. People are treated as change leaders, and in turn, that is how they will operate.

In this chapter we will look more closely at each level of the Continuum and how the deeper levels of engagement lead to successful change.

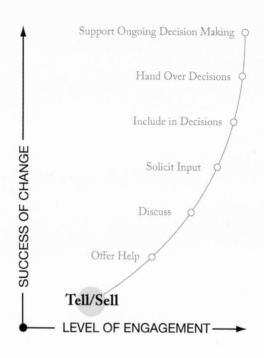

## Tell and Sell

At the low end of the Engagement Continuum, interactions are predictable and one-way, with a few change leaders maintaining control over the change and the people they want to change. This is the traditional method of instituting change. It consists of memos, communication plans, newsletters, videos, posters, and motivational meetings. The message is, "Here's the change, and here's what's in it for you." This level of engagement is necessary for any change – it conveys information and keeps people in the loop. But it is not sufficient to give people ownership for making change. Even seemingly innocuous changes will backfire if people feel powerless as a result.

Many years ago I watched an organization move a division from one floor to another. The move was orchestrated by consultants who wanted to increase the communication flow between departments and decided that the best way to do it would be to put the two departments on the same floor. They did their best to make the move smooth and prepared the floor carefully before anybody actually saw it. They had cubicles and desks custom built for the new floor and put street signs in the alleyways between the cubicles. They put little surprises on each desk – jellybeans, chocolates, colored paper clips, and beanie babies. They made a point of celebrating the move – that morning the head of the division gave a short speech, cut a ribbon they had tied across the entrance, and opened the floor for employees who were equipped with "street" maps to find their desks. The leaders and consultants (the change leaders) were happy with the move and felt they had handled it well.

The employees (the change targets), on the other hand, were miserable. They had all the information they needed. They were told what was in it for them – the easier communication, the upgraded computers, the better access to bathrooms. But they had absolutely no control. Everyone was assigned a cubicle. No longer were they sitting next to the people who had previously been their neighbors.

But that was not the worst part. The worst part was that the custom built cubicles were designed identically – with only one place to put their computers, one place to put their telephones, one place to put their files. There was no flexibility in the workspace. Left-handed people had to deal with a right-handed design and equipment placement. People who were used to customizing their workspace no longer had that opportunity.

To the small group of change leaders, this seemed like a small change for which they didn't need to seek input. For the people who were in the cubicles, it signified exactly how little they mattered and how replaceable they were. They lost control of the one thing they previously could control – their own space. The change was managed exclusively through Tell/Sell, without their involvement.

Again, I want to underscore that Tell/Sell is necessary and important to any change effort because it communicates the plans, intentions, goals, etc. that are driving the change – it's just not sufficient because it does not create people who change.

---

Tell and Sell activities include:

- Describe the change through emails, memos, videos, letters, and newsletters.
- Create communication plans defining who needs to communicate, to whom, about what, in what time frame, etc.
- "Sell" the change by emphasizing the advantages of changing to the people who must change.
- Deliver speeches with question and answer sessions.

---

**Offer Help**

The next level of engagement sends the message: "Here's how to change." At this level you provide instruction including trainings, job aids, frequently asked questions (FAQs), and some resources.

This level of engagement attempts to give people the knowledge they need to change. If customer service is changing, then people need to learn the new customer service skills. If the sales process is changing, then people need to know how to sell in a new way.

Like Tell/Sell, this level of engagement is necessary but not enough. A few initial leaders define a strategy and a few more plan how to help others achieve it. But many change efforts face resistance because people are told what to do (communication) and how to do it (training), but they are not engaged beyond that.

It is interesting how leaders often respond to this resistance. They use the same actions that created the resistance in the first place. They try to sell harder (more communication), and they lengthen training under the assumption that if people aren't complying, they must not know how. This is similar to giving someone a bigger meal because they didn't fully digest the first one. Initial leaders respond this way when they see people as change targets who must be changed. Once they see them as owners of the change – colleagues with whom they can collaborate – then they can access the tools further along the Continuum.

While helping people manage change is only the beginning, it is still an important part of any change effort.

---

Offer Help activities include:

- Create training programs to explain and provide opportunities to practice the skills needed for successful change.
- Develop forms and tools to help people change – along with trainings to learn how to use those tools.
- Dedicate people who can help others as they struggle with the change – help desks, telephone numbers in case of problems, etc.
- Disseminate frequently asked questions (FAQs) to offer solutions to ongoing problems or questions.

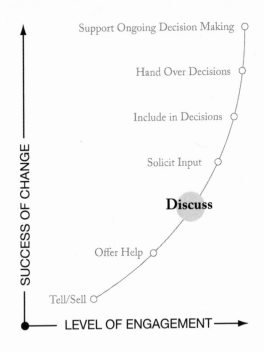

**Discuss**

As we move up the Continuum, the percentage of ownership increases as dialogue occurs. People are able to raise questions, and even express how they feel about the change. The message here is, "Are you OK? We do care." Change is about emotions as well as intellect; when emotions are engaged, people will follow.

This level is most often invoked to deal with some traumatic situation, like layoffs or a sudden relocation. People have to get things off their chests. In the previous example about the division relocating to another floor, this would have included bringing everyone together to talk about how it felt to move and to listen to their complaints: the feeling of loss at separating from people they had worked next to for years, the frustration at having to fit into a cubicle designed uniformly for everyone, the fear of carpal tunnel syndrome from having to sit and type in a certain way because of the placement of the computer.

This is an important step if done right because it brings emotion to the surface. I say "if done right" because in corporate environments emotion is often avoided in favor of a more acceptable intellectual response. "I can't do a performance review because I don't have the time with all my other priorities" is a lot easier and more accepted than "I am afraid to talk to my employee because I don't really know how." For people to express fear, they have to be willing to make themselves vulnerable. Without this willingness, real change cannot occur. You have to create a safe environment in which people can be openly imperfect.

R. D. Laing, a Scottish psychiatrist, defined hell as a place where there is intellect but no heart. Unfortunately this describes many corporations and change efforts. The strange thing is, it does not often describe the leaders of a change, many of whom are warm, caring people, sensitive to the emotional impact of change on others. But when it comes to writing the memo, running the training, or even facilitating an open discussion, they remain factual and unemotional. They submit to their perception of what is appropriate in a corporate environment.

I was watching the leader of a company talk to his organization about upcoming layoffs. This was obviously distressing to many people, some of whom would be losing their jobs, others who thought they might be next. This leader talked about the economic uncertainty, the drop in revenues and stock price, and the mandate by the board of directors to cut costs. He said that they had no choice and that this was necessary to keep the rest of the company strong. He was a polished speaker and he made logical arguments that no one could refute. But he did not show any emotion – he appeared strong and controlled.

After the speech, the two of us went into a room and he broke down in tears. "I feel terrible. I love these people. I don't want to let a single one of them go. They have families, mortgages. And they helped us grow." I listened to him for a while and then I asked him why he didn't show this side of himself when he was talking to them. "I want them to feel I am strong and will get us out of this." "That's an emotion too," I responded, "Why not show them both of those emotions?"

This man equated emotion with weakness. Nothing is further from the truth. Showing emotion takes great strength. Everyone else in that room felt similar emotions. Connecting with them emotionally would have strengthened his message. It takes a strong leader to express emotion and allow it to be expressed by others. This leader was a deeply caring human being. Showing others he cared would have only further engaged them in the process of turning the company around.

---

Discuss activities include:

- Create a safe environment where people feel comfortable expressing things that might not be popular.
- Be open to emotions as they enter the conversation.
- Avoid judgment about, or repercussions for, dissenting views.
- Coach to support people; help them feel taken care of during the change.
- Share your own emotion about the change; be vulnerable.

---

## The Engagement Continuum

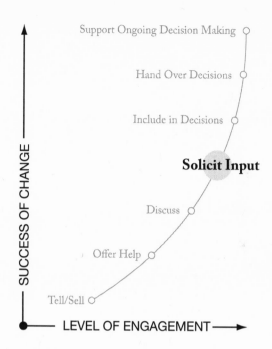

**Solicit Input**

The next level signifies the beginning of a shift that is the key to avoiding – not overcoming, but completely sidestepping – resistance. It is the level at which, if ever so slightly, control is shared. Here, leaders tentatively begin to ask people to join them. The message here is, "I care about your opinion and want you involved." People slowly gain control as they begin to feel ownership for the change.

A word of caution: better to remain at Level 2 or 3 than to posture at Level 4. Integrity is critical. If you are not open to considering the views of others, then don't ask for their input. You will only generate mistrust and resistance. Not asking might be bad. Asking with no intent to listen is really, really bad.

This integrity in communication is often an issue in merger situations. Don't say you are open to input for a decision you have already made. If you have decided to keep your Director of Human Resources – but the other executive positions are open – say it. Set your boundaries. If you act on their input in other areas, maintaining clear boundaries creates respect rather than resistance.

Solicit Input activities include:

- Ask for the opinion of others – and listen.
- Create clear boundaries about what has been decided and what remains open for input.
- Create vehicles for soliciting input – web sites, meetings, focus groups.
- Create space for people to discuss issues, think them through, and provide thoughts, suggestions, and feedback.

# The Engagement Continuum

**Include in Decisions**

At this point and beyond, the Continuum reflects the philosophy of extending control to the people who are ultimately responsible for doing and saying things differently. Make decisions cooperatively. As people are included, they will change.

This level of engagement is often used in the pilot stage of change efforts. Leaders conduct focus groups and try the change on a small percentage of the population. Pilot participants are asked for their involvement: to work with leaders to improve the change and make it more pertinent to them and their real issues. In other words, they are asked to be leaders themselves. And no one expects the change effort to be perfect or flawless. That would obviate the need for a pilot. Leaders are interested in the thoughts and decisions of pilot participants; they are truly curious about how participants will respond to it. Because they recognize that the thoughts, ideas, and decisions of participants will at the very least make the change better and at the most make it stick.

This is why most pilots are more successful than the full rollout. Not because it is harder to change 2000 people than it is to change 200; rather because the pilot engages people more deeply than the full rollout.

The problems arise after the pilot. By the time the leaders are confident enough to extend the change to 2000 people, they *know* the right way to do it and they know what will work. They are the leaders and see everyone else as targets. Their confidence gets in the way. Their knowledge prevents learning; it prevents them from using the higher levels of the Engagement Continuum. And it prevents others from being involved and taking ownership and making the change succeed.

The challenge is to run the entire change effort like a pilot. Don't seek all the answers – they will only get in the way.

Sharon Drew Morgan, author of *Selling with Integrity*, came to this same conclusion through trial and error – and developed her sales system accordingly and with great success. Sharon Drew was living in England and through a series of circumstances began to set up a computer business that she did not know much about. She wasn't clear on exactly what she was selling or what need she was satisfying.

So, somewhat reluctantly, she began to contact potential buyers and ask them what they needed. When they asked, "What are you selling?" she responded honestly, "I am not sure yet – I am still learning." Through these conversations, she convinced prospects that she really cared about meeting their needs. Her sales grew rapidly and she grew in confidence. At a certain point, she knew what she was selling and she created a pitch. She had the expertise. She knew what her potential customers needed and she could provide it to them.

But a funny thing happened. Just as her sales should have increased dramatically – after all she was now an expert – they actually dropped off. What she came to realize is that she no longer involved her potential clients in the process of solving their own problems. She was no longer facilitating the fulfillment of their need – she was selling from her own need. So she met resistance. The knowledge she had gained since she made those initial calls got in her way. Her challenge was to keep listening and maintain ownership where it belonged – with the buyer. In a change effort, ownership must belong to the people who are ultimately responsible for taking the actions that will make the change a success.

---

Include in Decisions activities include:

- Create imperfection; don't solve all the problems or make all the decisions before implementing the change.
- Create the boundaries of what cannot be changed.
- Create rules of decision making and stick to them.
- Make decisions together; ensure adequate discussion.
- Opt for customization over consistency (ensure that what needs to be consistent is in the boundaries of what can't be changed).
- Get support for yourself – it's hard to collaborate and share power.

---

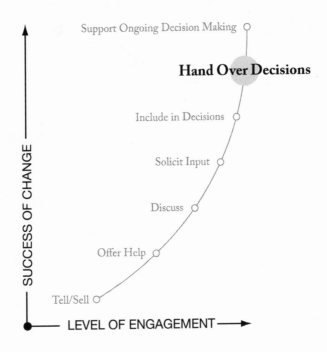

## Hand Over Decisions

Here is the point when the power of decisions belongs to the people accountable to implement them; to the people who must live the change.

Power lives in decisions. So everyone must make decisions that are critical to the success of the change. This is especially hard since initial leaders often have the deepest expertise in the change itself and think they know what the "right" decision is. But they will not succeed if they remain the only ones who own the change.

Everyone must live and apply the change everyday. The *process of making the decisions* is what buys people into a change and makes it succeed. Ultimately, their decisions are the right ones, even if they are not the ones the initial leaders made. This requires letting go of power. Letting people make "mistakes."

Sometimes people make decisions that seem downright wrong. That seem counter to the change. That look like resistance. Fine. Let them. If the boundaries are set appropriately, everyone will still move in the direction of the change.

Handing Over Decisions activities include:

- Create firm boundaries about what decisions can't be made by others.
- Let others decide everything else.
- Get support for yourself – it's hard to give up control.
- Support others in making decisions.

**Support Ongoing Decision Making**

The deepest level of engagement is when everyone can make decisions and ongoing judgment calls...permanently. In other words, the change belongs to them. To do with it what they will. This is the level of engagement that will ensure everyone changes and the change sticks.

A sales organization was struggling with a change and asked my company to bring in a number of consultants to lead the change. I counter-proposed that instead of my consultants, we use their internal people. They accepted and we immediately passed leadership from ourselves to two internal groups of leaders to ensure that we did not maintain control. One was a body of senior level people, presidents of the businesses, who were responsible to visibly support and model the change. The other was a group of internal facilitators representing each business unit and all levels of hierarchy. The members of these groups were business people – the leaders, managers and employees of the business. It was their responsibility to make the decisions about the change effort. To implement and sustain it. If they needed to change it, they had the power to. We facilitated the process with them. But the decisions belonged to them. We were advisors to their process. They were always in control.

---

Support Ongoing Decision Making activities include:

- Collaborate with others to create a process for addressing ongoing concerns.
- Provide resources and support to help others in making strong decisions.
- Ask, don't tell.
- Think with others and then ask them what they are going to do.

---

In Part II of this book, I will be specific about what you can do to achieve a deep level of engagement – to deepen the ownership, capability, and persistence of the people who will make change happen.

# Part 2:
# CREATING CHANGE

# 7 STRATEGIES TO CREATING CHANGE!

## STRATEGY 1: SHARE THE STORY

STRATEGY 2: KEEP EVERYTHING SIMPLE

STRATEGY 3: GET IT HALF RIGHT

STRATEGY 4: INTEGRATE THE CHANGE

STRATEGY 5: PROVIDE ONGOING SUPPORT

STRATEGY 6: BUILD IN FEEDBACK

STRATEGY 7: USE THE PARTNER SYSTEM

# Strategy 1:
# Share The Story

Every change needs, at its center, a compelling story. Why is the change being made? What will it achieve? How does it fit in with everything else people are doing? Why should anyone care? How do we know it will be successful? How do we know it will be worth our time and effort in making it successful? These questions are on everyone's mind, consciously or subconsciously. This strategy addresses the lower levels of the Engagement Continuum and enables people to understand the change and consider changing. It begins to solicit their ownership and, if told and retold, supports persistence.

I use the word "story" deliberately. I do not mean mission statement, which tends to be stale and dead. Nor do I mean goal which tends to be dry and linear. I mean story, with a plot and characters and excitement and emotion. Something that connects to a person's head *and* heart. Sure, a mission and a goal will be part of the story. But only a *part*.

## Appeal to Intellect and Emotion

Change is primarily an emotional issue; people wrestling with their loss of control, the possibility of looking stupid trying something they never tried before, the inevitable confusion that occurs when the future is unknown. Yet often leaders keep their communications on the intellectual level. "These are the three phases of the change." "This is the date of the move." "This is what you need to discuss with your employees."

A compelling story will humanize the change. It will appeal to people's sense of purpose. It will help them focus on what's really important. It will place the change in context – explaining why you are making the change and what you hope it will produce. It will inspire people with possibility. With hope. With passion.

## The Myth of the Burning Platform

I want to dispel the commonly held myth that people need a burning platform as a catalyst for change. The story goes that an oil-drilling platform built over the ocean in a freezing climate was on fire. Many people died. Some, however, survived by jumping hundreds of feet, braving the cold waters in which they only had minutes to live. When asked about their choice, the survivors said that they had no choice – that they were forced to overcome their fear of jumping and of cold water because the alternative was certain death.

The burning platform plays on fear. The fear that if they remain where they are – on the burning platform – they will be consumed by fire. Fear that something terrible will happen if the change is not made successfully. Fear that if the change doesn't work out, the company will die. Or they'll die. Or maybe they'll lose their job. This fear is considered a motivating force. After all, if you were on a burning platform, wouldn't you be highly motivated to get off?

But where would you go? When people are scared, they react. They become political. They try to protect themselves. They get stressed and sick. They look for other jobs. I am not an advocate of increasing fear during change.

Your role as you help people deal with change is to decrease fear not augment it. Fear leaves people feeling powerless and reactive. A good leader will work to motivate people positively, to offer them a compelling reason to buy into the need for change. Just not through fear. The story of how people are motivated is more complex than that.

## Social Motives

According to David McClelland, Harvard psychologist and father of social motivation theory, people are driven by a combination of three social motives: Achievement, Affiliation, and Power. Achievement is the desire to pursue challenges, win competitions, and reach increasingly difficult goals. Affiliation is the desire to be liked by others. Power is the desire to attain influence and status. Power is divided into Personalized Power and Socialized Power. Personalized Power is the desire to attain influence and status for oneself (e.g., the corner office, the important title, or the letters after one's name). Socialized Power is the desire to attain influence and status for other people (e.g., teachers, consultants, (some) politicians).

While every person harbors all three desires, they value each one differently. For someone high in Achievement, life is an exciting challenge. She will time the traffic lights on several different routes to work and choose the fastest one. In a traffic jam, she will drive in the exit lane, pass 10 cars, and then cut back in. She will use her cell phone so as not to waste time in the car. She has the spirit of an entrepreneur, willing to take risks in exchange for the rush of competition. Her steadily growing net worth is a measure of increasing skill and success more than buying power or status.

On a week long mountain bike trip in Utah, I met someone who always rode at the front of the pack. For the fun of it (and a little social experiment) I pedaled hard and passed her at a pace that I could only maintain for a few minutes. Sure enough, within 10 seconds, she sped past me. She chose not to be second. McClelland once said that he could predict an achievement-driven entrepreneur by the age of three. The more self-motivated his or her potty training, the more likely the entrepreneur.

A person high in Affiliation, on the other hand, sees the world in terms of relationships. He would never think of driving in the exit lane to pass other cars because he would not want the drivers to be angry with him. Unless, of course, he was late for an appointment, in which case he might even risk a ticket so as not to keep someone waiting. Generally, he would be so engrossed in conversation with his friend in the passenger seat (or on the cell phone) that he would not be bothered by the traffic. On the same mountain biking trip he would put little value on where he was in the pack, as long as he was in the pack. He would make sure to help out if anybody needed it. Most people on the trip would like him more than they would the woman out front.

A person high in Personalized Power might also be in the traffic jam, but she would be sitting comfortably in her Mercedes Benz or Rolls Royce. Periodically she would check her gold Rolex to see how long she had been stuck. She would certainly be on her cell phone because, frankly, she's that important. Also, she would be leveraging her contacts to ensure she maintained her influence. She would not feel particularly bad about being late to an appointment with someone "less important." However, she just might brave the exit lane not to keep someone of "higher status" waiting. When you met her she would want to know what you did and probably your title. She would notice your clothing, your accessories and the car you drove. Of course, on the same mountain bike trip, she'd have the nicest bike.

If she were driven more by Socialized Power, she might be the leader of the mountain biking trip. Still with a pretty nice bike. She would have specific instructions about what to do and not do and she would expect you to follow them. She would prefer your respect to your friendship. In the traffic jam, she would most likely be the police officer trying to keep the exit lane clear for emergency vehicles.

It is important to recognize that under the right conditions, all of the above people would be willing to drive in the exit lane. They might all be on their cell phones. They could all be on the same mountain biking trip. But for different reasons. And remember that everyone is driven by Achievement, Affiliation, and Power in varying degrees. A compelling story should address all three motives.

Successful change stories are consciously constructed. They are short, simple, clear, targeted, attractive, and personal. They are the scripts that make people want to be actors. Each story is unique; specific to the change, people, culture, time, and situation of each company. Yet there are certain elements every story should contain.

**Story Elements**

There are three major sections to a good change story: Content, Context, and Confidence. **Content** is the center, the focus. It's the main catalyst of the change. It describes the result you are seeking that will make the change worthwhile. **Context** sets the change in time and space. It describes how the change fits into the history of the organization. How it impacts each person and the company as a whole. It describes current reality and then physically places the change in the middle of that reality. **Confidence** is the power behind the change. It inspires action in its listeners. Invites them to join the change. It makes the change credible, offering assurance. The change *will* happen and it is a worthy place to lay one's bet.

## Content

This is focal point of your change: a **Challenging Unifying Goal**. It answers the question: Why change? It provides a challenge to inspire people. It indicates that we will achieve it together. It articulates the core purpose of the change; the result that will be achieved when the change succeeds. It's the lighthouse of your destination city. If you ever feel lost or indecisive or overwhelmed with the complexity of it all, you look up and see it flashing in the horizon.

It's one sentence long and it is your constant companion. This one sentence should appeal to all three social motives. For the achievement oriented, it offers a challenging goal. For the affiliation oriented, it offers a sense of community in achieving the goal. And for the power oriented, it defines how this change will make the company (and by extension the people working in it) truly great.

One insurance company that had 10 million customers in the year 2000 defined their Challenging Unifying Goal as: *We will attract 40 million happy customers by the year 2010.* 400% growth. Four times as many happy customers. And we will work together to attract them.

A retail company determined to improve the sales skills of their associates declared they were going to: *Improve the quality and quantity of client touch.* While this goal could be more quantifiable, it is rescued by its clarity.

In a financial services firm, customers complained about difficulty understanding and working with their technologists. The content of their goal was: *All employees will have effective performance reviews and opportunities to develop.* Every employee would be developed in an organization where previously only 50% met with their managers to discuss performance.

All these goals are clear, concise, challenging, and focused on an opportunity that everyone could pursue together. All these goals will instill a sense of pride and power in those who accomplish them.

**C** ONTENT
**ONTEXT** — Past, Present, and Future
**ONFIDENCE** — Individual and Organization

## Context

The context of the story situates it in time, **linking the past, the present and the future**. A good place to start is with current reality. What is the truth about the way things are at this very moment? How close (or far) are you from the Challenging Unifying Goal?

Then bring in the past. Where were you a month ago? A year ago? 5 years ago? What was it like in the "old" days? What's the legacy?

Then address the future. What will it look like? What do you want current reality to be when this change has succeeded?

The picture painted might be a straight line – from mediocrity to greatness. Or it might be a curve – from a great past to a mediocre reality to a great future. It's the time line of your story and it's inextricable from your plot. It is the cloth through which the thread of change is woven.

It is also important to **link each individual with the organization**. In this story, each individual involved in the change is an actor. Organizational change is a by-product of individual change. This relationship must be clearly articulated in the story. What is the role of the people who will make the change successful? How is each person creating the current organizational reality? How can each person impact the change? How does the organization – its structure, culture, processes, and politics – impact people's efforts to change. How has it in the past? How will it in the future? The story becomes real when it invites each person to see him or herself as an actor in the time and space of the changing reality.

## Confidence

People sometimes resist change because they lack confidence that the change will stick. Given that so many changes fail, this is a valid response. There are four major ways for your story to instill confidence.

### *Facts*

Confidence is generated, in part, by the feeling that leaders know what they are doing. If you are an early advocate of the change, you will be asked a million questions, all a variation of the following six: Who? What? When? Where? How? Why? And you will be expected to provide complete, well thought out answers.

There is a balance, though. As leader, you need to provide answers that communicate the critical components of the change and that convey to the organization that this change is serious and thoughtful.

But answers that are too complete are counter-productive. First of all, you can't possibly know all the answers because the change is just in concept stage. Many of the answers will come as the change unfolds. Pretending you have all the answers will generate suspicion. Second of all, because you can't possibly know all the answers, trying to provide them will inevitably lead you to some wrong answers. Acting contrary to those answers later will erode your credibility. And finally, if you do give all the answers, there is no room left for others to create their own answers. To write themselves into the change. You will be stuck owning the change and it will be an uphill battle from there. If they are the ones to make it successful, they need to provide answers.

Stephen King, in his book "On Writing," explains this well:

> If I tell you that Carrie White is a high school outcast with a bad complexion and a fashion-victim wardrobe, I think you can do the rest, can't you? I don't need to give you a pimple-by-pimple, skirt-by-skirt rundown. We all remember one or more high school losers, after all; if I describe mine, it freezes out yours, and I lose a little bit of the bond of understanding I want to forge between us. Description begins in the writer's imagination, but should finish in the reader's.

You need to set a clear direction while leaving room for others to complete the picture with their own thoughts, suggestions, actions, and decisions. The goal is to catalyze their creativity, not stifle it.

## *Truth*

By far the most critical piece of advice I can offer you is: *always tell the truth*. It is the most important element of the story. This is non-fiction. It is naturally exciting because it has yet to unfold. The suspense is real. By all means, plan the story carefully – omit the details that are unimportant, include the information that will inspire passion and desire – but do not in any way lie or even slant the truth. Resist the temptation to spin. You will be discovered and you will lose all credibility, as will the change. Even if you are not directly exposed, people will sense something and they will no longer trust you. You cannot trick people for long. You certainly cannot trick people into becoming passionate, creative, diligent leaders and actors of change.

If you are unable to construct the story using any of the elements I have described so far (the change is too ambiguous, you don't understand it, you have no goal, you can't figure out how the customer fits in, you cannot see the past, present or future, you are confused by the link between the individual and the organization), then be honest. That takes courage but it creates an immense amount of goodwill that will take you and the organization the rest of the way.

A friend of mine, Beth, has a 1½-year-old baby girl, Jennifer, who became ill with a stomach bacteria and had to take a very strong and foul-tasting medicine called Flagyll. Those of you who have children know that you cannot force a baby to eat something.[1] If she doesn't want it, she will simply spit it out. You also know that if the baby wants to put something in her mouth, she will. Very much like people

---

[1]     *Actually, you can. You force their mouth open, hold their nose, and stick the spoon or syringe way into the back of their throat. Since they can't breath without swallowing, and you're preventing them from spitting it out by introducing it past the spitting muscles, they eventually swallow. It requires two or three adults, and years of therapy afterwards. I don't recommend it.*

during change. Beth tried very hard to disguise the taste. She had the pharmacist double the normal amount of fruit flavoring. She mixed the medicine in with foods Jennifer liked. She smiled when giving it to her and pretended that everything was normal, even happier than usual. Nothing worked. In fact, before she even tasted the medicine in the food, Jennifer knew something was off. She would scream, cry, and wiggle away. But she would not take the medicine.

Then Beth tried a completely different approach. She told Jennifer the truth. She was not at all sure that Jennifer would understand; the verbal comprehension skills of a 1½-year-old leave a bit to be desired. But she went ahead and explained the situation openly and honestly. "Jennifer, I have to give you medicine because your tummy is sick. I know this medicine tastes awful. And I feel terrible every time I give it to you. But you need to swallow it four times a day and it's the only thing that will help you get better. I am sorry it tastes so bad. I don't know how to make it taste better."

Jennifer stopped crying and looked directly at her mother. She opened her mouth and took the medicine.

Now, when Beth takes out the medicine, Jennifer actually helps her. She puts the dropper in the bottle (it takes her a few tries) and squeezes it to suck the medicine in. Then she sits back and waits. She still screams and wiggles at the point when the dropper enters her mouth. But only at that point.

It doesn't matter that Beth meant well; that her intention was honest. Jennifer resisted because she somehow sensed that her mother was not being truthful. Her mother's deception caused more pain and resistance than the medicine on its own. Once her mother shifted to being open, direct, and honest, Jennifer immediately settled down. The entire process was less painful.

Honesty, even in terrible situations – especially in terrible situations – will generate respect and support.

### *Why It Will Succeed*

The story should clearly explain why the change will succeed. If someone thinks the whole endeavor is doomed, they'll never choose to support the change. Who wants to captain a sinking ship? I have often seen people maintain the stance of "waiting out" the change. "This is the third performance review system in the last three years. Next year, there will be another one. I think I'll wait until then." For a change like layoffs or a merger, the stance might be: "Why should I bother to get involved? They'll never listen to me anyway. I'll just wait and see what happens (meanwhile I'll put out my resume)."

In this case, being honest is critically important to building that credibility. If there were three diversity programs rolled out in as many years, admit it. And then say why this one is different. Or say, "I don't know that this one will be different. Only time will tell. But if these new tools make it easier for you to run your teams or your businesses, then use them. And if you use them, this change will last longer than the others. It's up to you, not me."

Explain why the chances are better this time around. "We've learned from the past, so these new performance reviews are two pages long, not 10." Tell them how the new CFO has led turnarounds at three other similar companies. Tell them how the two CEOs from the merging companies had three disagreements and explain how they worked out those disagreements (as a model for how they will deal with challenges in the future). Tell them how important this change is to the leadership and how they will see the leadership modeling the behaviors they are asking the rest of the organization to demonstrate. And mean it.

## *Role Model*

Instead of relying on a burning platform to scare people into seeing change as a priority, use your commitment. Devote time, money, and people power to it. You have to do that anyway if you want the change to succeed. Create systems of accountability that communicate seriousness. And, most importantly, model the change. That is part of the unspoken story that communicates more than anything. Don't hold other people to it until you publicly hold yourself to it.

The senior leaders at one of our clients hired us to roll out a new communication program and they were outspoken supporters of everyone else communicating more openly and consistently. But when it came to their own communications, they were inconsistent. Employees began to resist the change; they became suspicious of its longevity and wondered whether senior leadership was posturing. The leaders were faced with a stark reality – either they needed to publicly support the change by living it themselves, or it would not happen. They chose to stand behind their commitment. Not only did they agree to communicate openly with the rest of the organization on a regular basis, they also agreed to publicize their compliance on the company intranet. That public commitment clearly and undeniably sent a message to the rest of the organization that the change would be supported and was here to stay.

One of the reasons people do not support a change is that they believe others won't either. They don't want to be the first one to contribute. They don't want to look stupid if it fails. Role modeling is the part of the story that tells people they will look more stupid outside the change than inside. It gives confidence to people that they are not alone.

I watched an example of this in an organization during a change of leadership. When the old leader moved on, she left behind a group of very loyal followers who were not interested in seeing their new leader succeed. The change was a hard one as factions broke off and actually plotted to overthrow their new leader. It reminded me of how we responded to new teachers in the eighth grade – it was a point of honor to get the teacher to quit because we were so badly behaved.

I discussed options with one of the ringleaders. She could continue to fight, and maybe even win, and then what? Would she do the same thing when the next leader arrived? Was she happy in this fighting mode? Did she want it to continue from one leader to the next? And what exactly was in it for her? After several conversations, she decided that it was more in her interest to support this new leader. She changed her attitude. It took courage because she risked being ostracized by her teammates.

But that is the role of a leader. To take a risk for a higher purpose. So that others know they will not be alone when they make changes. One by one the others shifted their stance. The balance began to tip. Soon, it was socially riskier to fight the leader than to work with her. The fighters no longer looked like courageous loyalists, they looked stubborn.

Modeling the change means being sensitive to perception; to how others interpret actions. A woman I met at a conference told me this story: The CEO asked her to articulate the company's values to all 450 employees. She created a committee to define the values, brought people together to discuss them, and finally worked with the CEO to design a big bang launch. As planned, they threw a party with banners, food, drink, speeches, music, and even Karaoke. The CEO was on stage singing Karaoke with the rest of them – celebrating their respect for people (one of the values) and integrity (another of the values) with fanfare. Three days later, the CEO laid off 30% of the organization.

Everyone must be clear about and aligned behind the final story. When hired to help a client execute change, one of the first things I ask is, "How aligned is your senior leadership?" Almost invariably, I am told that the senior team is on the same page. I used to believe that answer and simply move to the next step. Not anymore.

One of our clients was experiencing a series of changes. Their primary objective was to leverage the opportunities of the Internet. At the same time, the organization was experiencing new leadership and office consolidations. Some positions would be eliminated, with many of the employees repositioned; others would be relocated. Meanwhile, managers and employees needed to stay motivated and serve clients.

In our early meetings we agreed on our story. The company was a leader in using other cutting edge technologies years before anybody else. They would continue that tradition of innovation on the Internet. No burning platform. No fear tactics. The opposite actually: inspiring people with the story that they are part of a proud tradition that they must now continue.

I was assured the leadership team was on the same page regarding not only the story, but also the strategy for achieving the goal of the story. I pushed, but again I was assured of their alignment and warned that rewriting the story would put people off.

When we opened the meeting with an overview of the change capabilities we were planning to teach, questions bubbled to the surface. How big is this change? Which areas will be impacted? What results exactly are we supposed to produce? Who is part of the change and who is outside it? What do we, as leaders, need to do? It quickly became clear that they didn't need skills, they needed a story.

The story was not clear, the strategy was not defined, and the leaders were not aligned. We had to quickly shift gears and design plan B: create the story together in that meeting. One by one each leader stood up and articulated his or her version of the change. Collectively, their stories led to a deeper discussion of the strategy. These internal leaders developed the strategy only after they had created a compelling story based on what they knew, believed, felt, and heard.

If you find yourself struggling because there's so much to tell, because the change is so all-encompassing and complex, read the next chapter.

# 7 STRATEGIES TO CREATING CHANGE!

STRATEGY 1: SHARE THE STORY

STRATEGY 2: KEEP EVERYTHING SIMPLE

STRATEGY 3: GET IT HALF RIGHT

STRATEGY 4: INTEGRATE THE CHANGE

STRATEGY 5: PROVIDE ONGOING SUPPORT

STRATEGY 6: BUILD IN FEEDBACK

STRATEGY 7: USE THE PARTNER SYSTEM

# Strategy 2:
# Keep Everything Simple

In the late 1990's Xerox reported a serious drop in earnings. As the Wall Street Journal reported:

> Xerox has blamed some of the woes on disruption to its sales force following a reorganization announced earlier this year that puts more emphasis on selling services together with machines. *The shift required Xerox's 14,000 sales employees to spend more time in training and development than in selling products.* Friday, Xerox said the restructuring continued to affect "sales productivity." (Emphasis mine)

Sales people couldn't do their jobs because they were too busy being trained to do their jobs. Hmmm.

Keep everything excessively simple. Prioritize. Focus only on the most important aspects of the change. The one behavior that will make the most difference. The one skill that will generate deeper communication between employees and managers. The one action that will increase organizational performance. The more narrow the focus, the better the chance that people will do it – and the faster and more economically it will be accomplished.

Like the previous strategy, this one focuses mostly on the lower levels of the Continuum by giving people the right kind of help so they can use it to make change. It does, however, contain a bridge to the higher levels of the Continuum which I will point out later in the chapter.

What seems simple to an expert in the change will probably be unnecessarily complicated for action-oriented everyday people. Experts are deeply involved in the change, speak the language, and study the concepts. Others don't care about the academic nuance. And if they do, they'll seek it on their own.

A few months ago we held a day long meeting with one of our clients. Together with their Human Resources people we created an innovative new training and development initiative. We included Just-in-Time (JIT) trainings, 360° feedback, skills coaching, and several other elements. Everyone seemed clear and ready to move forward as planned.

At the end of the day we presented our work to several people who had not been part of the planning. They listened carefully, nodding. We were sure they were impressed. Then one particularly brave nodding woman said, "I can see you are all excited about this and I am very happy about that. But I haven't the foggiest idea what it all means." I am certain that if any of our "end-users" were in the room, they would have felt the same way. We spent the next day simplifying it all.

Complexity creates an unnecessary wall between people

and the change you want them to make.

Simplicity is not easy. The beauty of minimalist art relies as much on what is left out as on what is included. With too much clutter, the important elements are hidden, accessible only to the skilled.

The irony is that most organizational clutter is created to compensate for lack of skill. Step-by-step instructions on what to do each minute of a performance appraisal conversation. Re-engineering that includes minute detail about the execution of a process. This sends a clear message to people: "You don't need to think. Frankly, we don't trust your judgement. Just follow the steps exactly as they are outlined." And even if the result is mediocrity, at least it's predictable, consistent mediocrity.

The penchant for complexity in corporations seems to be getting worse. Processes that only a few people fully understand. Implementation plans that need to be followed precisely if the result is to be achieved. The assumption is that people can be trained to follow the process. The problem is that they are trained for only that: following a process. Not communicating more effectively, not managing with more skill, not developing their ability. And then what happens when something changes? The entire system risks becoming obsolete.

Instead, we must make everything easier, more reliable. Help people develop new habits, simple habits, that begin to change who they are. One small step at a time. We don't want people to follow a communication process. We want them to be communicative. We don't want people to follow a process map of a customer interaction. We want them to care about the customer.

The first step? Simplify learning so people can develop their capability.

## Simple Learning

Minimizing the need to acquire more knowledge can be the most effective way to simplify change. Focus on *applying* knowledge instead of just *acquiring* it.

Traditionally, trainings are long and teach hard-to-apply concepts and theories. We already know that 90% of the people who go to training do nothing differently afterwards. Effective learning seeks to change one behavior at a time. Choose the one behavior that will make the most difference; that will drive action and results. This simplification and prioritization is critical to the success of the change.

To ensure consistency, many organizations want everyone to learn the same thing. All new managers get management training. Everyone in a merger goes through the same culture orientation training. That model is organization-driven rather than individual need-driven. Better to customize learning for each individual. Develop objectives with people and then ask them what they're missing; what do they need to learn to achieve those objectives? Trust them to know. If several people need to achieve an objective together, have them assess the skills they are missing as a team. Then you can support them with exactly what they want to learn. One of the problems being faced by corporate training departments is low attendance – people cancel at the last minute because of something "more important." If they choose what they want to learn, they will come.

People should never spend more than half a day in training. They won't remember more. Give up fine distinctions. Training is often designed around what trainers want to teach, not what people can absorb and act on. Teach the main point and prepare people to use it.

A half-day training can be a catalyst and a culture builder. A way of setting up expectations and sharing a common language. A way of communicating the change to everyone.

I designed a template for this high impact catalyst called Just Enough To Start (JETS™). It is never more than four hours, of which only fifteen minutes is spent learning new material; the rest of the time is spent grappling with it or planning to use it in daily work. It's designed to move people from concept to action in six steps: (1 - Learn) learn about the new behavior, skill or ability; (2 - Watch) see it demonstrated; (3 – Question) ask questions, wrestle with it and come to own it; (4 - Try) practice it; (5 - Plan) plan in detail how you can use the new behavior, skill or ability in the next week, and (6 – Get Feedback) offer and receive support from others.

# JETS™

## Just Enough To Start

Introduction

Learn

Watch

Question

Try

Plan

Share Feedback

Closing

These steps are simply good learning practice. The trick is to keep it simple and focused. Set a foundation for learning that is not dependent on the classroom. Teaching people *how* to learn is even more important than teaching them *what* to learn. In JETS™, people learn with each other and develop relationships they can leverage for future learning.

Following is the outline of a sample JETS™ on Customer Service:

---

## Introductions (15 Minutes)

---

**Content**: Participants introduce themselves and describe a time they received great service.

**Comments**: Relationships among participants are an important result of the JETS™. Most learning happens in conversation and action with others; the connections developed during an event are critical to changing behavior after it.

In the customer service training, for example, ask participants to describe a time they received great service. This will enable them to visualize the goal and recognize that they already know what it takes to deliver great service. This is about action more than knowledge.

---

## Learn (20 Minutes)

---

**Content:** Describe the learning objectives and identify the one critical behavior for the session: empathy. This behavior must be connected with the story we discussed in the last chapter – applying the behavior will lead to achieving the Challenging Unifying Goal.

**Comments:** First, motivate the topic and give context by offering a broad brush stroke of the change and describing the learning process: how it works, what results people can achieve, and what they will need to do to achieve those results. Define a common language for the participants.

Next define the behavior: "Empathy is demonstrating an understanding of the customer's perspective, interests, and needs to *their* satisfaction." Participants will learn to give their customers the experience of being heard. That's it. That one behavior will create a service-oriented culture.

They know exactly what will be expected of them and they won't waste their time. If they want to learn more, they can ask for it or pursue it on their own; self-motivated learning is a huge asset. They are accountable for their own development which they will achieve in the course of their work, not in a classroom.

---

## Watch (15 Minutes)

---

**Content:** Show them two examples of empathy.

**Comments:** Offer examples of the behavior in action, for example a video or role-play of someone using empathy in a difficult customer interaction. This supports visual learners and helps everyone by presenting a model of how the behavior looks when performed effectively. It helps people visualize their goal.

## Question: (25 Minutes)

**Content:** Does this apply to you? What seems difficult? Impractical? What wouldn't work? How can you adapt this material to your own situation and needs?

**Comments:** While all steps of the JETS™ help participants increase their capability, some sections, such as this one, reinforce ownership as well. Allow participants time to process, digest the material, disagree, and own it themselves. This is a perhaps the most crucial piece of the training because it gives people the opportunity to mold the material for their own use. If empathy doesn't fit their particular circumstance, ask them what will and encourage them to make changes to fit their need.

This step is the bridge to higher levels of the Continuum; it's where participants begin to customize the change for themselves.

## Try (45 Minutes)

**Content:** Participants practice empathy while role-playing real situations they have dealt with in the last month or need to face in the coming week.

**Comments:** In small coach-guided groups, they practice the new behavior. They practice listening, responding, solving problems, dealing with irate clients, etc. They make mistakes, learn from their mistakes, and most importantly, ask each other for help. They not only learn empathy, they learn how to learn together.

## Plan (45 Minutes)

**Content:** Participants write plans for interacting with empathy on the job.

**Comments:** Supported by a roving coach, they each create a SMART (Specific, Measurable, Achievable, Results-Focused, and Time-Bound) plan to apply the new behavior in real life. Coaches guide people to ask and answer a variety of questions that generate commitment to act. When and where will they have the opportunity to implement the new methodology? In what situation over the next week can they try the new behaviors? What results are they looking for? What obstacles do they expect? What contingency plans can they create? This step, and the next, develops and reinforces all three attributes of people who change: capability, ownership, and persistence.

## Share Feedback: (60 Minutes)

**Content:** Participants share plans and feedback in small groups.

**Comments:** This solidifies the learning group concept. Discussing their plans in a group fortifies their commitment. They ask each other challenging questions, offer ideas, and give each other support. They choose learning partners and agree to check with each other in a week.

---

## Closing (15 Minutes)

---

**Content:** Motivational speech about taking action.

**Comments:** Reinforce that their development is not about *knowing* something; it's about *doing* something. Success is in the attempt and reattempt.

It is essential that any training is followed with weekly coaching, learning groups, or some other form of action support, addressing questions such as: what worked? What didn't? What obstacles appeared? What options exist for circumventing them next time? What will be done next week?

## Other Ways to Simplify

While I emphasize the importance of simple, useful learning, there are other ways to keep change simple.

One client of ours relied heavily on a concept called "sunsetting." This client was going through a change in the way they went to market – selling different products through new channels. Everyone was overworked as they maintained their everyday tasks, added on the work required to leverage new channels, and helped each other manage through the change itself. Each person listed everything he or she did in a day, prioritized it, and "sunset" the bottom 20%; they simply let it go. You know what? Nothing was lost except the guilt of not having enough time to do everything anyway. Everyone could then focus on his or her top priorities.

Role modeling is essential to simplifying. If senior leaders and "C" level executives (CEO, CFO, CIO, CMO, etc.) aren't doing it, then no one else will. I was working with a

CFO who complained that everyone in her organization was a perfectionist. "We have too much to do here – why would people spend three days trying to get my signature on a letter before sending it out? They should just send it out themselves! And why do they spend so much time making sure that everything is perfect? I don't care if I get a letter with a typo in it. I would rather get the letter with a typo today then get a perfect letter tomorrow. Speed is the most important thing." I asked her if she ever sent out a letter with a typo. "No, but I work faster than everybody else does." We decided she should role model imperfectionism. She agreed to send out some letters with typos – typos she placed in there herself – to make the point that people should move fast and allow for errors. This might seem like dangerous and unnecessary modeling – but it increased the speed and decreased the stress in that organization dramatically. And it kept the priorities simple – speed is number one.

One word of warning: Simplicity might engender resistance in some experts. A client of mine who ran human resources in a small company called me up, clearly disturbed. She said that she had contracted with another consulting firm to redesign their performance appraisal form and process. Over the course of several months, the consultants had interviewed a number of employees, held focus groups, reviewed the old system, conducted a benchmarking study, spent a few weeks designing, and finally, earlier that day, had given her their final work product. "They billed me a fortune and it's a disaster," she said. After her requisite apologies for having not given the project to me, she asked me if I would review the work and give her some suggestions.

We met the next day over breakfast. By the time I arrived she was already on her second cup of coffee. I sat down apprehensively. What was she going to show me? What disaster would I have to untangle? Would I be able to? She leaned over and, with a little disgust, handed me a very thin folder and said, "This is the total product of their work from the last 3 months."

There were only 3 pieces of paper in the folder. The first page was a letter to managers and employees describing the process and offering a few hints for communicating safely and openly with each other. The second was an appraisal form with 5 competencies on it. The third was a form for creating a plan for the following year – including space for development activities and dates when they would be accomplished.

It was actually one of the best, most simple and direct performance appraisal and development forms I had ever seen. It had the essential elements, but no more. It reminded me of the sentiment expressed in the last line of a very long letter written by Mark Twain which said something to the effect of: "I am sorry this letter is so long but I did not have the time to write a shorter one."

I handed it back to her and said, "You know, it takes a lot of time and courage to whittle something down to its core components. You're right that you could have done this yourself. But you asked them to do it and they did a great job. I wouldn't touch it. You've put enough money into creating it. Now spend your money implementing it. Put your effort into getting people to use it as a tool to speak with each other honestly and clearly. It's great because it's simple enough that it shouldn't get in their way."

# 7 STRATEGIES TO CREATING CHANGE!

STRATEGY 1: SHARE THE STORY

STRATEGY 2: KEEP EVERYTHING SIMPLE

STRATEGY 3: GET IT HALF RIGHT

STRATEGY 4: INTEGRATE THE CHANGE

STRATEGY 5: PROVIDE ONGOING SUPPORT

STRATEGY 6: BUILD IN FEEDBACK

STRATEGY 7: USE THE PARTNER SYSTEM

# Strategy 3:
# Get It Half Right

I heard a story a few years ago that's a great metaphor for effective change. The leaders of a newly built university campus could not decide where to lay the sidewalks. They argued about where students would walk, to which buildings students would use shortcuts, and how students' walking habits might change from year to year. After too much time speculating, they landed on a brilliant solution. They gave up. They chose not to create sidewalks at all. Instead, they planted grass throughout the campus. Then they waited and watched. After a year, they saw where the grass was worn down to dirt. That's where the students were actually walking. So that's where they put the sidewalks. They set the boundaries (the buildings) and then let the students define the strategy (the sidewalks). Students were perceived, and treated, as the owners and leaders of the change.

Think of the advantages. On the front end, they averted a huge expense that would have been based on incomplete data (who really knows where the students would walk?). On the back end, they avoided trying to control student behavior with signs and chain posts to keep people off the grass. Students felt empowered because the decision was based on their needs.

What did it cost them? Nothing; they saved money by laying sidewalks one year later and only doing it where necessary.

It is equally important to create firm boundaries and to stay flexible inside those boundaries. Prioritize. Ask, "What's the underlying objective? What is not essential to that objective? Where is the space for people to make their own choices about how to achieve that objective?" Smart people want to know where they're headed but they don't want to be told how to get there. Let people choose their own path for achieving the objective.

This strategy moves the change effort towards the higher levels of the Continuum – where people make their own decisions, based in their capability and sense of ownership.

In a financial services firm where we implemented a performance review system, our objective was to improve communication and employee development. We were charged with the task of using the performance review process to ensure that managers and employees talked to each other so that employees knew where they stood and where they were going.

After simplifying everything as much as we could – the forms, the language, the behaviors that needed to change – we shortened the training from a one-day session covering everything, to a few short JETS™ workshops, each offered Just-In-Time. We gave people just the information they needed precisely when they needed it.

Here's the most important thing we did – when they

came to the sessions, we told them a little about the change and what was expected of them, showed them the forms, and demonstrated good communication. Then we invited them to complain. That's the step I called "Question" in the JETS™ model described in the last chapter. It's the most important step in gaining commitment to change.

We didn't try to sell them. We didn't ask them what they liked about the change (e.g., ask them to sell it themselves). We asked them what they thought would prevent it from being successful. We asked them to do what they were predisposed to do anyway. To prove us wrong. To complain.

And complain they did:

"This form is too long."

"There is no way to collect all that feedback in the time allotted."

"How am I supposed to have a conversation with an employee I never see?"

And the list went on.

While we felt we could answer many of their complaints, we didn't. We could have jumped in with a little hand-to-hand combat and we probably would have won. Intellectually at least. But in the end, we would have lost because we would have put them in the role of change target and, over the years, change targets have mastered the art of passive resistance (they've gotten a lot of practice through all the previous programs that are long gone). Next time you are trying to convince someone of something – stop and ask – do you really need to? Or can you find another solution?

Compare two martial arts: Karate and Aikido. In Karate, if someone punches me, I block it. I do this by stepping forward and using my arm to intercept their punch. It's an aggressive move. My next move is even more aggressive. I throw a punch back. We continue like that – facing off against each other, throwing punch after punch, block after block, until one of us can't take it anymore. In the end, we will probably both get badly beaten.

In Aikido, if someone comes at me with a punch, I don't block it with force and I don't throw a punch to meet it – rather I step aside. I spin around so that the punch misses me and I end up standing side-by-side, cheek-to-cheek with my opponent. I move with the energy of the punch and reinforce the direction my opponent is taking. Neither of us gets harmed. In the end, I have spun around so that I am no longer facing my opponent; rather we are facing the same direction. Sharing the same perspective. I have removed myself as an obstacle. Now we can look together from the same vantage point.

When people objected to the changes we were asking them to make, we did not try to convince anyone we were right; that the change was strong and research-based; that it had worked in other companies; that the rewards couldn't come without their discipline and effort. We just listened.

And then, to their surprise, we agreed.

If they saw obstacles to making this change work, they were 100% right. Because *they* were the only ones who *could* make it work. To become owners of their performance review system, they had to see their own way through the obstacles.

After a while, we said, "It sounds like you think this change won't work. It will be a real time drain and you don't even have the time to do the things you are already supposed to do. Plus you think it's too complicated." And we continued to describe all the problems.

Then we said, "You're right – redesign it with us, right here, right now." And we engaged them in problem solving with us. Together we came up with a series of improvements that individuals could apply as they needed to. We knew the boundaries of the change – certain things couldn't be touched. But in reality, most things could.

"How about we restrict our comments to the greatest strength and most glaring weakness – and leave everything else blank?" Great idea.

"How about we only ask five people for feedback instead of eight?" Fine.

"I'm not the right one to give this person feedback, but Cheryl is." OK – talk to her about it and make sure she agrees.

And so it went. They were impacting the change by making it work for them. We had to remain incredibly flexible. We had to let go of our view of the ideal change so people had room to write themselves into the "story."

We were able to bend the rules because we knew our "story" well. We knew our objective was to help people communicate. We could help them evaluate each suggestion with that objective in mind. Will this help you communicate or make it more difficult? If breaking a rule will help you communicate then go for it, break the rule. Liberate yourselves from having to implement a program.

THE PROGRAM ISN'T
THE POINT.
THE POINT OF THE
PROGRAM IS THE POINT.

Let people decide what they need to do to achieve the intended result. If your change plan doesn't help, let them come up with an idea that will. The plan is only a tool to help people get a result.

We didn't just make these changes in a pilot and then rollout a "perfect" change to the rest of the organization. Each and every training was a working session in which new participants molded the program to meet their needs. *People owned the end result of communicating with their employees because they redesigned the change specifically to meet that objective.*

Some of you might be thinking, "If you had designed the change correctly the first time, you would not have had so many complaints." Perhaps. But you *want* the complaints. You *want* to design an imperfect change. You are *aiming* for 50% or 60% perfect – not 100%. Perfection is impossible. Attempting perfection is costly and the illusion of perfection is dangerous. If you think you have it right, you end up being invested in your *program* rather than the *purpose* of your program. Most of all, you rob people of their most valuable incentive – their own creativity, ownership and involvement in customizing the change to their needs.

One thing I hear people say is, "Even if I create a perfect program, I am still open to new ideas. I still ask people what will make it work for them and I am willing to listen. Often they don't know the thinking that went into the program – and when I address their concerns, they seem satisfied." I mentioned this to a friend of mine who is a teacher, author, and gardener. She specializes in helping things grow. Not growing them. Just giving them enough good dirt and water, questions and ideas and then letting them grow themselves. Her response: "A program that is completely thought-out is slick. It's never really perfect, it just seems to think it is. And slickness has a certain stench of its own. People can smell it. And they know they can't impact it. It belongs to the author, not the reader."

I have developed a five-step coaching model to help people redesign, customize, and own their change. I use this model during JETS™ (in the "Question" step described in the previous chapter) and after JETS™, during coaching sessions (described in Chapter 10, Provide Ongoing Support). Using this model keeps others in the driver's seat, where they stay in control at the high end of the Engagement Continuum. For a mnemonic, combine the first letter of each step to spell: the QUICC™ Coaching Process.

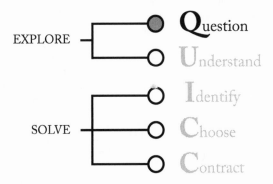

## Question

At first we simply ask people: what works? What doesn't? If they respond by asking clarifying questions, we give them the clearest answers we can. If they don't challenge us or ask questions, then we pose more questions. Our goal is to engage them in a detailed discussion about the change effort, the new behavior, our expectations, their expectations, the methodology, etc. What do they think? In which situations will it work? In which situations will it not? What's wrong with it? What will be difficult to apply?

Through our detailed questioning and their specific answers, they increase their knowledge of the change and uncover challenges or obstacles that might arise during implementation. It is critical not to judge, argue, or defend. Simply pay close attention as they process the material and uncover their own issues. Let them say what they want. Take it in.

We do not probe deeply at this point. We do not ask "Why questions", such as "Why will that be challenging for you?" These questions come in the next step, "Understand."

If you ask them now, you might get defensive or slip into an argument. It's tempting to judge the validity of their concerns. Your job is simply to surface the issues, not solve them.

It is important that your questions come from a place of curiosity. From an honest desire to draw out their thoughts and opinions. I was watching one person ask questions of a group and she said, "You don't *really* believe that's going to be a problem, do you?"

That wasn't *really* meant as a question, was it?

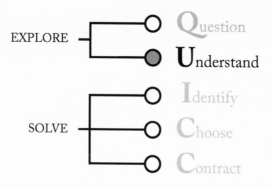

## Understand

Once we have built trust by listening to their concerns, we increase their self-observation by exploring what's underlying their thoughts. This is a time for reflection about the problems and their seriousness. Why will something be a problem? In what way will it be a problem? In what kinds of situations? How big an obstacle do you think that will be?

In our work rolling out performance reviews I remember someone in a workshop who raised his hand and said,

"Look, in the 15 years that I have been in this company, I have never received a performance review. Why should I give a performance review to my employees?" I stayed silent for a minute to allow what he had just said to sink in and to ensure that I wasn't responding in defensiveness. Then I asked: "Would it have been helpful to you during those 15 years to have had an honest and forthright discussion with your manager about your performance?"

It was not a rhetorical question. I was asking because I wanted to hear his thoughts and I wanted him to hear his own thoughts.

"I guess it would have," he said, "but I never expected to get one."

"Well," I said, "you have to make a personal decision. Do you want your employees sitting here in 15 years feeling angry that they never got a review or do you want them to receive direct and honest feedback now? What kind of a relationship do you want with the people you work with? What kind of manager do you want to be? Ultimately it's your choice." I asked him to think about it and then choose.

"I want to be a better manager to my employees than my manager was to me."

This step is critical in fostering the three attributes of people who change: ownership, capability, and persistence. Here people begin to get involved, feel ownership and develop capability. As they explore their concerns, they clarify the change, inspecting each piece to assess whether they can buy into and act on it. And they delve more deeply than if we had simply listed the change on a flip chart or played games to learn the new information. They aren't just listening, they're wrestling; thinking critically and making judgments and decisions about what to keep, what to eliminate and what to add. They own the learning process.

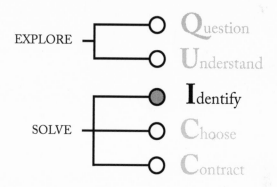

**Identify Options**

Now we switch modes: from exploring the problems to solving them. Here, our attention is on discovering alternative ways for people to achieve the underlying objectives. The alternatives don't have to work for the whole company. Or the 2000 people in a single division. Or even the 400 in the business unit. Just the people in the room.

The more *you* are able to make solid decisions based on achieving your underlying objective, the more *everyone else* will make judgments in the same way. The converse is also true: the more you focus on following an exact program, the more likely you will get people who follow the program but miss the point.

We always identify at least three options for every problem. Two options and they might feel they are between a rock and a hard place. And while we can *help* them come up with options, it's *their job* to come up with them.

So, back to the manager, I asked him what his options were.

"One option is to give all my employees performance

reviews. I want to be a good manager but I don't have a lot of time so maybe I could review only some of them – the ones who really need help. Or I could review all of them and only point out their weaknesses, though I guess that would hurt morale. So maybe I could review all of them and point out one strength and one weakness."

He created several options from which he chose his own action.

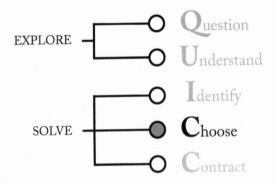

## Choose One of the Options

After identifying the options, we examine how each one will support the underlying objective. We go back to the "story" that was developed earlier, paying particular attention to the Challenging Unifying Goal. Which option will most strongly support the achievement of that goal? This of course reinforces the idea that everything we do is in the service of the results. At this stage we get very specific – what actions will each person take to achieve the results. Again, not everyone needs to do the same thing.

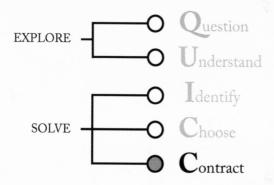

EXPLORE — Question
Understand

SOLVE — Identify
Choose
**C**ontract

## Contract

What specifically will each person commit to doing, by when, in what way? Here we make sure that actions are SMART: Specific, Measurable, Achievable, Results-focused, and Time-bound. The more concretely people commit to act, the more successful they will be.

In a very short time, people have learned about the change and, more importantly, they have redesigned it to fit their needs. They own the change.

# 7 STRATEGIES TO CREATING CHANGE!

STRATEGY 1: SHARE THE STORY

STRATEGY 2: KEEP EVERYTHING SIMPLE

STRATEGY 3: GET IT ~~HALF RIGHT~~

STRATEGY 4: INTEGRATE THE CHANGE

STRATEGY 5: PROVIDE ONGOING SUPPORT

STRATEGY 6: BUILD IN FEEDBACK

STRATEGY 7: USE THE PARTNER SYSTEM

# Strategy 4:
# Integrate the Change

I once asked a sales trainer why she didn't actually sell with the people she trained. She paused for a second, I guess judging how honest she should be. So I looked back at her warmly. It obviously worked because she said, "I know how to teach this stuff but I am not 100% sure that it works in practice. Honestly, I would rather teach it and if they don't do it – it's their problem, not mine."

She was in the expert paradigm: if her model didn't work, she failed. But if she stepped out of the expert paradigm and into the partnership paradigm, she would welcome it not working. She would see it as her opportunity to ask deeper questions, transfer ownership, and help people devise their own strategies – incorporating the best of what she knew and the best of what they knew. Together they would succeed. *Ideally, there should be no separation between learning and working.*

This strategy supports people in capability and persistence by seamlessly weaving the change into their day-to-day work and creating an environment that supports them.

Traditionally, most organizational change occurs in the form of change *programs, initiatives, implementations, or trainings*. If the goal is to communicate better, an organization will launch a performance review program. If the goal is to increase sales, a company will do it through a sales training focused on the new sales behaviors. If the goal is to grow rapidly, someone will call it a version of "the Grow-Fast-Now initiative." Creating change as a program, initiative, or training is tempting because it contains the change – clearly defining its beginning and end.

But the reason it's tempting is also the reason it doesn't work. Once the program ends, so does the change. If the change is important enough, it should not be a separate initiative. It should be part of people's everyday work. An organizational change should, in fact, change the organization. Not just during the program, but permanently.

Last year, millions of people in America bought diet books or participated in weight-loss related programs. My mother is a great example. She recently called me to tell me that she is going on the Scarsdale diet. "What? Why?" I asked. She said, and I'm quoting her here, "In the last week I've gained 5 pounds." 5 pounds in 5 days. I said, "That's impossible. Either your scale is broken or you drank 5 pounds of water right before you weighed yourself the second time." She insisted that she had gained the weight and she did indeed go on the Scarsdale diet. Three days later she called me back, excited. "This is the most amazing diet in the world."

Now, I should tell you that my mother would know the most amazing diet in the world because over the last 20 years she has been on most of them. Recently, she spent months drinking a tomato and spinach soup. When I was a child I remember her (and, incidentally, me) eating steak for breakfast, guided by Atkins' initial diet revolution. When she was on Fit for Life, she carefully combined foods so as not to cause her stomach the challenge of processing carbohydrates and proteins simultaneously.

I should also tell you that my mother is not overweight. She has looked pretty much the same over the last 20 years – she is a beautiful and glamorous woman.

"I have lost 5 pounds so far and it has only been 3 days. Well, Mr. Know-It-All, diets never work, eh?" Being the ever supportive and humble son I said, "I must have been wrong. Congratulations. Call me in a week." A week later, at my brother's birthday dinner, over her second helping of Carvel ice cream cake, she told me that she had regained the weight that she had lost, but she was "going right back on the diet" after dinner.

Why don't these diets ever work? Losing weight couldn't be simpler – we all know how to do it. Summed up in four words: Eat less, exercise more. So why is it so hard to *do*?

Let's go back to the three attributes of people who change: capability, ownership, and persistence. She has the capability, though apparently not at the Carvel moment. She seems to have the ownership – nobody told her to lose weight; she made the choice on her own. The persistence, however, is lacking. She follows her diets strictly . . . until dessert. Her lapse in persistence costs her the result. After berating herself for being weak, what does she do? One of two things: she goes back on the diet or she gives up on the diet, gains more weight, and then after several months chooses another diet (one that is sure to work!)

I see this behavior in companies all the time. Managers aren't managing well. So the company buys a new leadership methodology (a philosophy, a training program, maybe little wallet cards that remind people how to lead) and teaches it to all their managers. A year later, managers still aren't managing well. If the company doesn't give up, they buy even newer leadership methodology and teach it to their managers. Perhaps the new one is competency-based, or uses mentoring, or focuses on high potentials, or grades people and fires the lowest 10%. This one will surely work! The cycle continues. Nine times out of ten, the problem is not the methodology. It's the failure to integrate that methodology into people's day-to-day work.

When my mother is *reading* her diet book, she is 100% committed to losing weight and eating exactly what the book tells her to eat. But when she is sitting at dinner and everyone is eating cake, she loses that commitment. It's easy to be a good leader during a leadership training class. But what about when you are dealing with an employee who always comes in late to work? Or someone whose performance is substandard? Or when you are tired, overworked, and annoyed? That's when you need the reinforcement.

By integrating the change into work, decisions become easier. If ice cream is not a dessert option, I won't eat it. A fully integrated change means that my environment completely supports the new behavior. No ice cream, no problem.

The next best integration is when support is provided at the point of decision. For example, let's say my father attached the following note to the Ben and Jerry's pints in their freezer: "Check out the fresh raspberries in the fridge." When my mother opens the freezer, she immediately gets the support she needs. She already knows that fruit is a healthier snack than ice cream. She just needs a reminder that the raspberries are there and that she is the sort of person who cares and acts on this information. Integrating that support into her life helps her persist.

Most managers already know what they need to about

leadership. Whatever they don't yet know can be easily taught. But at some critical point (usually the most challenging point), they don't use that knowledge. Their environment does not support it. Or they need a reminder. Most change programs put their emphasis on sharing knowledge. Using a training, email, memo, etc. to communicate what people need to do differently. But they rarely help them do it at the right moment.

CREATE AN
ENVIRONMENT THAT
SUPPORTS THE
CHANGE

That's the challenge: Create an environment that fully integrates and supports the change. Erase the line between change and work. The following is a process to help. Usually the leaders who initiate change use this process, but there is no reason why each person can't use it to integrate the change in his or her own life. Again, the more each person does him or herself, the more he or she will gain the ownership, capability, and persistence to make the change stick.

O **What behavior needs to change?**

O **When does it need to change?**

O **What's happening now?**

O **Choose the changes.**

O **Choose the opportunities to integrate.**

O **Integrate the change.**

O **Add new opportunities.**

Every change must result in someone doing or saying something differently. Otherwise nothing has changed. What specific behavior needs to change? If someone needs to lose weight – what do they have to do? If they need to negotiate – what exactly must they say or do to be effective? At this point you do not need to consider people's capability to change. You only need to know the ideal behaviors that will define that someone has changed. Write a list of all the behaviors that will demonstrate excellence in this change. It's too soon to decide what's appropriate, what's too overwhelming, or what will realistically work. That comes later. Do not censor or judge yourself here – feel free to be inclusive and expansive in what needs to change.

○ **What behavior needs to change?**

○ **When does it need to change?**

○ **What's happening now?**

○ **Choose the changes.**

○ **Choose the opportunities to integrate.**

○ **Integrate the change.**

○ **Add new opportunities.**

When should the behavior manifest? At what point in an interaction should someone demonstrate these behaviors and who else is involved? Most changes require some shift before, during, and after an event. If the change is weight loss, then what has to happen before a meal (bring your own dessert?), during the meal (make healthy choices) and after the meal (review your choices, get real time feedback – for example, how do you feel after the second piece of ice cream cake?)? If the change is better negotiation skills, then what has to happen before a negotiation (understanding your own needs, desires, and boundaries), during a negotiation (empathize with their needs, assert your own, brainstorm options), and after (debrief, maintain a strong relationship with the other party, follow through on commitments)? Place the behavior in time and space; in the real life context in which it will be demonstrated.

○ **What behavior needs to change?**

○ **When does it need to change?**

○ **What's happening now?**

○ **Choose the changes.**

○ **Choose the opportunities to integrate.**

○ **Integrate the change.**

○ **Add new opportunities.**

Create a behavioral diagram of current reality. If the change is weight loss, then what is actually happening before the meal (you haven't eaten anything for 12 hours), during the meal (you grab the first thing you can get your hands on), and after the meal (you feel sick and you swear never to eat again, which you do for 12 hours until the next binge strikes)? If the change is better negotiation skills, then what is happening before the negotiation (maybe nothing, maybe you decide what you want from the other party), during the negotiation (you get angry at your "opponent" for being so inflexible), and after the negotiation (nothing)?

This picture is a blow-by-blow account of the reality in which change will be integrated. In it is hidden all the opportunities for supporting or reinforcing the change.

○ **What behavior needs to change?**

○ **When does it need to change?**

○ **What's happening now?**

○ **Choose the changes.**

○ **Choose the opportunities to integrate.**

○ **Integrate the change.**

○ **Add new opportunities.**

Now is your time to be realistic about what needs to change. Look at your list of all the behaviors that will demonstrate excellence in this change and then ask: Which of these *need* to exist for the change to succeed? Which can I give up for now? If the change is losing weight, the most important behavior might be a food journal; write down everything you eat. For negotiation skills, the behavior might be to prepare by comparing your needs, perspective, and interests to theirs. As you know from the previous chapters, the less people need to change, the better. Cut out as much as you can. If the first step (What behavior needs to change?) was your first draft, this is your edited second draft.

Perhaps, if you are a catalyst for the change, you are the wrong person to make the decisions of what should change – perhaps you are too intimate with the change and it all seems important. This is the perfect opportunity to involve others more deeply and climb higher up the Engagement Continuum. Let them choose the one or two things they can do differently that will have the most impact on their performance. You are not giving up on the other behaviors. You are simply prioritizing; choosing a place to begin.

At this point you have finished defining the change. Now you are ready for integration; for embedding the change in the nooks and crannies of a workday – the small spaces and opportunities you can leverage to shift behavior right when it needs to shift: at the point of action.

○ **What behavior needs to change?**

○ **When does it need to change?**

○ **What's happening now?**

○ **Choose the changes.**

○ **Choose the opportunities to integrate.**

○ **Integrate the change.**

○ **Add new opportunities.**

This step involves using every available opportunity to communicate and reinforce the change. Popular opportunities exist in every communication, whether it's written or spoken. Some written examples could include: email, fax, letter, newsletter, video, role-description, task list, post-coaching write up, questionnaire, employee survey, focus group write up, weekly reports, new hire orientation packet, or performance review form. Some spoken examples could include telephone, conference call, meeting, speech, video conference, training, coaching, mentoring, brief conversation, off-hand comment, focus groups, staff meeting, new hire orientation, or performance reviews.

Since your goal is to integrate this change into existing work, you should leverage the opportunities that are already there. The more you can rely on what already exists, the less disruptive and time consuming it will be for everyone.

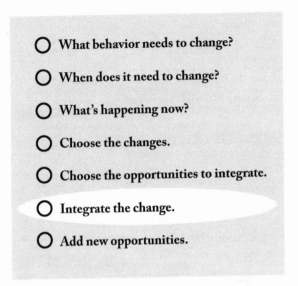

○  **What behavior needs to change?**

○  **When does it need to change?**

○  **What's happening now?**

○  **Choose the changes.**

○  **Choose the opportunities to integrate.**

○  **Integrate the change.**

○  **Add new opportunities.**

Once you have identified the opportunities that already exist, decide which ones to use to communicate the change. For clarity and consistency, any changes should immediately be incorporated into the material already used on a daily basis in the organization: role descriptions, performance reviews, new hire orientation, weekly update emails. You don't want to tell people they should sell in a new way and then measure them differently in their performance review. If you initiated the change, you might use existing opportunities to communicate to the entire organization. If you are newer to the change, you might leverage opportunities for your team or even for yourself – send yourself reminder emails, add a new goal to your performance review.

To the extent that you can avoid extra paper, extra meetings, extra emails – avoid them. Your best opportunities exist in work that is already being done. If the new behavior is facilitating meetings, then change the weekly staff meeting to incorporate the new methods and facilitate it with a coach. If you are teaching people (or learning) to empathize with customers, teach them (learn it) while on the phone or on the floor with customers.

For one client I designed a process where sales people routinely asked customers for feedback on the sales floor. Incorporate the change as a habit in daily schedules. Reinforce the change through already occurring conversations, staff meetings, and coaching sessions. If a morning email is sent out to all sales people, make sure the change is reinforced in that email. Integrate as much as possible into existing opportunities.

Rely on people who are part of your organization before looking outside. HR generalists and specialists, line directors, managers, supervisors, and employees can all be instrumental in delivering the messages and catalyzing the behaviors of change. People who are already in conversation with each other should deliver key messages and teach new behaviors.

Only once you have exhausted your existing opportunities to integrate the change should you begin to create new opportunities.

---

O   **What behavior needs to change?**

O   **When does it need to change?**

O   **What's happening now?**

O   **Choose the changes.**

O   **Choose the opportunities to integrate.**

O   **Integrate the change.**

O   **Add new opportunities.**

---

In traditional change, this is the first step. Create a new training. Bring in consultants. Create a video. But in reality it should be the last resort – only to be used after all other steps are complete and all existing opportunities exhausted. After integrating everything you can, look to see what is left over. What could not be communicated using existing opportunities? What behavior could not be changed or reinforced? Look at those few things and devise a plan for integrating behaviors *as close* to the point of action as possible. If you plan to use coaching – do it right after or right before action. If you plan to rely on training, make it a JETS™ and only teach what cannot be learned during an event. Be succinct, quick, and targeted. People need to be on the floor doing the work.

By this time you will have found ways to integrate most of the learning into existing opportunities. Adding a speech here or a JETS™ training there should be minimal extra work – for everyone. Once you have defined what needs to be added, ask yourself whether you have the internal resources to accomplish those tasks. Do you need the external legitimacy of a consultant? The external knowledge? Fine. But use the consultant to help you build your own capability and ownership as well as your organization's.

That's the process. Translate the change into a few simple behaviors, clarify exactly when the behaviors must be demonstrated, find the opportunities to spread the change during normal day-to-day activity, use existing opportunities to introduce, teach, and reinforce the change and only then, add extra opportunities to pick up the slack.

I used a version of this process when I helped an organization of thousands of people remap everyone into new roles. Previously the organization had hundreds of different titles. Now they were reducing them to 14. Managers had to look at the new role definitions and place all their people into the new roles. When they approached me to do this work, they were planning to train people in the new roles and then ask them to match fake case study roles into the new ones. Then, once they had some practice, they were to go back to their offices and, over the next few weeks, map all their employees. This would obviously take time away from their work and didn't adequately prepare them to address real issues. In pilot groups managers saw the training as a waste of time and felt unprepared to do the mapping by themselves. Compliance was low.

Instead, we decided to use training time to do the actual mapping rather than do fake case studies of the mapping. The whole point of the reduction in numbers of titles was to increase transparency. Great, let's start by getting the managers together in one room and doing the mapping as a group. Any issues that arose would be discussed and resolved together. Coaches supported managers by asking the kind of questions that managers needed to consider as they did the mapping. Managers could ask coaches to help them with difficult cases. Their work and learning were integrated through an existing opportunity – their mapping training. Instead of wasting their time, we were saving them time, effort, and struggle.

After completing their most difficult mapping cases, managers planned their ensuing conversations with employees about their new roles. We didn't role-play a pretend case; we practiced their expected conversations. First, our coaches took the manager's role, and the manager took the role of the person he or she would have to speak with. That way, managers could really get into the mind-set of the people they were managing; they could feel their employees' frustrations, arguments, and expectations. Meanwhile, they watched their coach handle the conversation skillfully by listening and speaking with integrity and compassion. They were able to witness the conversation they suspected was most likely to go awry . . . go well.

Then we switched and the manager played him or herself; the coach, another employee.

This process not only transferred capability, it provided integrated support in absorbing and applying new skills *while* working, not *in addition* to working.

Integrating the change takes careful planning. When done successfully, it results in a seamless relationship between learning and doing. This process works because the most effective learning is really a process of discovery. Applying information you already know. Using skills you already have. If you already know all these things then why haven't you applied them? Part of the answer is found in this chapter: you can break your old habits by redesigning your environment; working the change into your schedule, processes, and practices.

The other part of the answer lies in the next chapter. Someone who is expected to change needs specific support to make those changes;  support that helps them discover their strength and capability before action, helps them reflect on what they did after action, and plans for the next action.

# 7 STRATEGIES TO CREATING CHANGE!

STRATEGY 1: SHARE THE STORY

STRATEGY 2: KEEP EVERYTHING SIMPLE

STRATEGY 3: GET IT HALF RIGHT

STRATEGY 4: INTEGRATE THE CHANGE

STRATEGY 5: PROVIDE ONGOING SUPPORT

STRATEGY 6: BUILD IN FEEDBACK

STRATEGY 7: USE THE PARTNER SYSTEM

# Strategy 5:
# Provide Ongoing Support

My wife Eleanor and I used to live in Princeton, New Jersey, in a small house divided into three apartments, each with its own parking space. We had two neighbors, one of whom was a very intense professor – we'll call her Leslie. She was smart, lively, and very opinionated. We had not gotten into many conversations with her, primarily because they often evolved into debates and we inevitably lost. Truth be told, she was a little scary to both of us.

One night we returned home from a movie very late to find that there was a car parked in our space. We were tired, the movie was not particularly good so we were annoyed, and we were not feeling all that tolerant. The Princeton police will not hesitate to ticket an illegally parked car so we had the car towed, parked our car in its rightful space, and went to sleep.

The next morning there was a loud knock on the door. Now I should tell you a few things. First of all, both Eleanor and I have taken classes in communication, mediation, and negotiation – skills that we had had plenty of opportunity to practice with each other in our first few years of marriage. We knew all about the importance of empathy and assertiveness – hearing and being heard. We were both pretty good at it, actually. Secondly, I had been regularly working with a coach – someone with whom I spoke at least once a week and who was invaluable in helping me apply the knowledge I already had in situations where I was so challenged that I forgot to apply it.

So, there was a knock on the door. Eleanor was the first to answer and once she opened the door she immediately regretted it. There was Leslie – beet red as though she had been holding her breath for the past 10 minutes. In fact, she might have been because as soon as she saw my wife a trail of angry words and accusations burst out of captivity from her mouth. I was in the back of the house but I could hear her clearly.

"How could you have done that to me? I can't believe you could be so callous. So incredibly rude. I always thought you two were nice." And on and on. Now Eleanor was taken aback, her adrenalin kicking, and she did what any of us might have done when confronted by a charging bear. She defended herself. "What are you talking about?" She said. Well, it turns out it was her son's car that we had towed! Well, Eleanor and Leslie went at it – both arguing their points. Meanwhile, I had a 45 second conversation with myself. It went like this:

"What will diffuse the professor?" I thought for a second – "She needs to be heard." "How can you do that for her?" I asked myself. I thought for a second. "I can ask her questions and repeat her answers until she sees that I understand how upset she is." "Good," I coached myself, "Don't try to make your point until she's diffused – she'll never get it. Once she relaxes her shoulders, then make your point."

I took a deep breath, felt my adrenaline pumping, and joined the fray. They were both angry at this point.

"What's up guys? Leslie, you seem really angry about something." She saw a new victim and pounced. I listened. "Wow," I said, "I can see how angry you are. Your son only visits once in a blue moon and you really want him to have a good experience when he's with you. And then the people who you think are your good neighbors have his car towed. One more reason for him not to come home."

"Yeah, that's right," she said, indignantly. And then she was silent. She had nothing else to say because I had understood the depth of her reaction. She was heard. At that point I could tell her we were sorry. That because her son came so seldom we did not recognize his car and there was no note on it. And we needed to park. She got it. Thanked me for understanding, suggested that she communicate with us when her son is coming home, and returned to her apartment.

I want to stress that had I been the one to answer the door that morning, it would have been me, not Eleanor, under attack, and I would likely have found myself in defensive mode as well. The advantage I had that morning was the time to coach myself at the very moment I needed it – at the point of action. I had the knowledge to respond but because this was a surprise attack and a challenging situation, I would have been unable to access it without pausing, breathing, thinking, and coaching myself. That was the difference between competently applying knowledge versus passively holding it.

Eventually people are able to support themselves. But in the beginning, it is critical that they receive external support over time to work through their obstacles and challenges.

ANY SMALL CHANGE YOU ASK OTHER PEOPLE TO MAKE IS A BIG CHANGE.

This strategy addresses the highest level of engagement – Supporting Ongoing Decision Making – and it reinforces all three attributes of people who change – ownership, capability, and persistence – especially persistence.

Ongoing support over time is often neglected because it's risky. It involves helping people apply the concepts they learn. Sure they work in theory. But as Jan L.A. van de Snepscheut once said, "In theory, there is no difference between theory and practice. But, in practice, there is." Support is about helping people apply their new skills, knowledge, or business process over time, in the face of real life obstacles, dilemmas, and competing priorities.

That's where coaching comes in. Coaching is my personal favorite way of getting support over time. It is a process through which a person discovers his or her natural ability for higher performance. The role of the coach is to expand awareness (enabling the person being coached to "see" outside their normal habits of action), to focus on areas where change will have the greatest impact, and to practice that which is discovered in the process. A good coach seldom "instructs" or tells someone what to do. Instead, through skillful questioning, the coach helps a person use his or her own natural or learned ability to change. As a result of coaching, the individual uses new competencies, skills, and habits so they become second nature.

To truly grow a capability people need to move from Awareness (what is this thing I am trying to do differently?) to Accountability (it is my responsibility to do it differently; I will do it differently), to Action (I am doing it differently in this situation). The coaching process moves a person through that cycle: from Awareness, to Accountability, to Action.

When we teach people to do something new, it's important that we continue to check in with them, to see how the application of their new skill is going, to work through obstacles, and prepare for continued action. Coaches deal with real issues, real time.

To coach for ongoing support, use the same five steps of the QUICC™ Coaching model I described earlier with a slightly different focus. In the facilitation sessions during a JETS™ training, the focus is on helping people deepen their understanding of the change, wrestle with their own issues, and customize it to their own needs. In a coaching session, the goal is to help people move to action as quickly as possible.

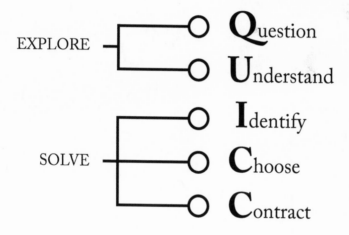

Coaches guide people to become aware of what they are doing, saying, feeling, and thinking in a given situation (Question), clarify which of these actions are helping the situation and which are making it more difficult (Understand), identify at least three options for changing action based on the need of the person, the situation, or the overall environment

(Identify), choose the specific actions they can commit to doing over the next week (Choose), and specifically and measurably contract to take those actions in the designated time frame (Contract). Following are some examples of detailed questions that coaches can ask in a QIUCC™ Coaching session:

### Question Reality

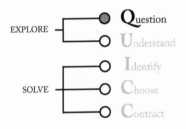

- What is actually happening now?
- Do a F.A.S.T. assessment:
  What are you...Feeling?
  How are you....Acting?
  What are you...Saying?
  What are you...Thinking?

### Understand Impact

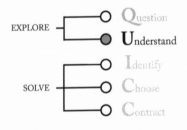

- What's working? What's not?
- What behaviors helped/ hindered success? (Increase self-observation)
- How are your actions supporting or detracting from the organizational change?
- What kind of feedback and responses are you getting from others?
- What patterns can you see in your behavior that are helping or hindering your performance?

### Identify Options

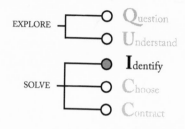

- What outcomes do you want to produce?
- What can you do differently to produce those outcomes?
- What are at least three options for things you can say or do differently?
- What are the pros and cons of each option?

### Choose an Option

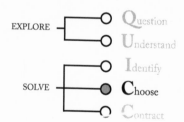

- Given the options, which do you think will have the greatest impact?
- Which will keep your actions positive and on track with the results you are seeking?
- What are some contingency plans if the options don't pan out?

**Contract for Action**

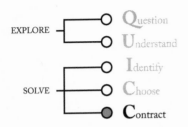

- What will you commit to do over the next week?
- Are the actions S.M.A.R.T. (Specific, Measurable, Achievable, Relevant, Time-bound)?
- How will you measure success?
- How and when will you have feedback on whether it is working?
- What do you need to take this step?

People leave a coaching session committed to making specific changes that will produce better results. The coach guides the process, asking questions that focus a person toward action. After a while, the people being coached begin to ask themselves the questions, focus themselves, and learn from reflecting on their experiences.

A study conducted across a variety of training subjects concluded that training followed by coaching increased productivity by 88%. By contrast, training without coaching increased productivity by 22.4%. The bottom-line: coaching increased productivity more than 300% over training alone. For this reason, we always follow training with coaching.

Relying on coaching allows you to drastically shorten training and ends up being cheaper and faster than training alone: development time is focused on work that needs to be done and people get back to work faster. Learning doesn't have to start, finish, and take root all in one session.

While coaching often works with one person at a time, it can be a useful tool with groups as well. First, it's cheaper, because seven or eight people can work with a coach at one time. Second, by coaching people collectively (in a room or on a conference call), you reinforce the learning culture; people practice thinking and learning together. Third, you help colleagues network and build relationships that might help them in their future work. Fourth, in a group, people recognize that they are not alone; others are feeling, experiencing, struggling, failing, and succeeding in the same way they are. Fifth, people can use each other's strengths to overcome their weaknesses.

The downside is that in a group setting the people being coached do not get as much individual attention, and the sessions cannot be confidential. Sure, everyone will agree to ground rules and one of those will invariably be that what happens in the coaching session will stay among the group. Let's be realistic though; there are sometimes lapses. And even if everyone religiously upholds that rule, there are still seven or eight other people in the group who are listening to your issue. So if someone wants to keep a problem, struggle, issue, or question completely confidential, they need to speak with a coach individually.

That said, there are very few things that *need* to be confidential. One of the nastiest problems I see in organizations is when people keep confidential what should be spoken about openly. In fact, bringing the confidential into the open is an effective group coaching technique.

The CIO of a very successful company asked me to help him with his senior team.

"What's the problem?" I asked.

"They don't get along," he answered.

"And why is that a problem?" I asked. He paused and looked at me a little strangely, wondering whether he made the right decision by calling me in.

"Isn't that obvious?" he asked.

"Not really," I responded, "Lots of people don't get along and it doesn't interfere with work. What are they doing or saying that is causing a problem?"

He thought for a minute. I sat in silence. Finally he smiled. "It's not what they are saying and doing that's the problem. It's what they aren't saying and doing."

"Go on."

"They don't collaborate."

"Meaning?"

"They hide. The angry ones, the vindictive ones – they withhold information that others need to know. The people who don't seem so angry – they just don't share information with others. I don't think they're holding back on purpose, I think they're trying to come in, do their work, and leave without involving themselves too much. Without getting in the way and exposing themselves."

"Can you be really specific with me?" I asked, "Let's go through a list of all your senior people and tell me what each person is doing, or rather not doing, that is getting in the way of the group's success."

" I'm not sure that's a great idea," he responded.

"Why not?"

"Well, I'm not sure it's fair to expose them. To identify or tag them as problems. It doesn't feel right to name names."

Do you see the problem? On a superficial level, people were sabotaging each other by withholding information. They weren't playing nice in the sandbox. On a deeper level, they were not talking about the problem. The CIO was actually modeling the problem by withholding information from me. If their leader, the CIO, was unwilling to be open with a confidential outsider, I was pretty sure people were not discussing the problem openly with each other.

As is often the case, the opposite of the problem is

the solution.

I agreed to work with the group under the conditions that I could coach them as a group and that they would all commit to being in a room together for two full days. Normally I would never keep people in a room for so long but in this case we would be opening a Pandora's Box, and stopping the process before handling the sensitive issues would have backfired. He agreed and we set the date for two weeks from our conversation. During those two weeks, I spoke with each member of the team individually in order to understand the problems from their point of view. Some were more courageous with the truth than others, but they were all cordial and willing to speak with me. All but one. Shelly cancelled our meeting twice. We did not speak before the session.

The morning of the first day, the group gathered at a downtown hotel conference room. Shelly was the only one missing. We spent the morning playing some team games. I was watching to see how people interacted. They were watching to see how I handled them, assessing whether they could trust me. I had built trust with each of them on the telephone but this was different. They were a group now. They were vulnerable.

After the games, they saw that I was trustworthy. They had offered me confidential information, and I kept it confidential. I didn't embarrass anyone. They began to relax.

We sat around the table and I introduced the coaching process. "Thanks for coming today and for committing to be here for the full two days. You might be wondering why I required two full days. We cannot start this process without finishing. We will get ugly in here but we will emerge safely and much happier on the other side. Are you all in agreement to stick with this for the two days?" They hesitated, asked a few questions, and agreed. I gave them a short overview of the QUICC™ model and launched into the initial stage,

"Question." I gave everyone a full pad of sticky notes.

"This is the point at which we ask questions. Lots of questions. Any question you have that you want answered. Every single one of you has questions that you are not willing to discuss openly. Questions about the leadership of this group. Questions about each other's commitment to this group. Questions about each other's competence. These are not questions that you have openly raised and discussed. They are questions you have left in the closet. *I will not "out" you.* You have all shared things with me that I will not share with others, but you can and must share them with others now. In front of each of you is a pad of sticky notes. Please write one question per sticky note and use up your entire pad. You might think your questions are stupid, or dangerous, or will never be answered. That doesn't matter. Write them down anyway. Hand them to me and I will anonymously post the questions on the wall. Once they are all up, we will read them, discuss them, and understand them. Our number one goal is to put all the "undiscussables" on the table. Then, we will discuss the "undiscussables."

There was silence. Could they really trust the process? Would it really help to get all the questions out in the open? Would they get to the other side intact?

They started writing. Their first few questions were polite, but by the middle of the sticky note pad they were running out of easy questions. Towards the end of the pack they each began to ask the important, dangerous ones:

"Why was John promoted to Vice President?"

"Sam (the leader) doesn't share information openly." (OK, it wasn't a question, but the point was clear and needed to be discussed.)

"What do we need to do to get more resources for the internet project?"

And the biggie: "Where's Shelly?"

One by one we discussed these questions. Some we dispensed with quickly, others we sank into, moving slowly through awkward silences. As their coach, I kept the conversation going, kept the space safe, avoided blaming, and helped people open up. I guided them to respect each other's feelings without using that as an excuse to avoid the truth.

By the second day, they didn't need the sticky notes or the anonymity. Over the course of the two days, they learned to openly ask each other hard questions, accept responsibility for the role they each played in a situation, and overcome their fear of speaking out loud the murmurings they had previously kept behind each other's backs.

During those two days, no one could really answer the question "Where's Shelly?" They called and emailed but she never answered. When I finally reached her she said that she was not interested in all this touchy-feely stuff. I reminded her that she had lots of complaints about others in the group. This was her opportunity to air them and work toward a solution. "I am not interested in a solution. Frankly, it's not my problem; it's theirs. Let them find a solution. I am perfectly happy."

Shelly returned to work after the off site, but having missed the two days, was playing by the pre-off site rules; a game that no one was willing to play anymore. When she tried to speak about someone behind his back, she was told to speak directly to the person. When she complained about something, she was asked what her role was in the problem. A couple of weeks later, she left the company. The new environment did not support her work style.

During the off site, people learned the coaching process: ask questions, understand the issues, identify options, choose actions, and contract with each other to do something by a certain date. Trust was built as they fulfilled their contracts and did what they said they would do. I continued to coach them as a team, and then individually, to support their progress.

After a few months, we slowed the coaching to an "on-call" basis; they were capable of managing themselves. Our work was successful because we did it as a group.

Ongoing support includes more than just coaching. It includes anything that helps people stay focused on the change; that helps them consistently do and say things that will move them forward.

In creating a plan for ongoing support, consider:

**Resources**: Are people supported with the resources they need to change successfully? To answer this question, think about when and where they might need the support. On the phone with a customer? On the sales floor? Right before a conversation with an employee? Look at how the change is now integrated in people's lives. What resources do they need to act? Do they have the software? The trainers? The help line? The books? The mentors? The money to access all of the above right when they need it?

At one client, everyone in the organization was given a $100 credit at Amazon.com to purchase whatever books they felt would support them over the year – whenever they needed it. A small price for a strong message of ongoing, personalized support. One resource always in short supply is time. If the change requires time, will they have a specified time in which to accomplish it? If they have to learn a new behavior, do they have to watch online tutorials on their computers at night? If they have to fill out a new form, do they need to squeeze it into their already too full day or is there something being removed from their day?

**Priorities**: Is the importance of the change clearly and continuously communicated? Organizations sometimes move too fast for their own good. How many different priorities cross your desk? Every quarter? Every month? Every week?

Every day? It's hard to keep track, right? It's not just the program-du-jour. It's the everyday "emergencies" that take top priority "just for the moment." After enough moments, there's no time left for the strategic priorities.

I have experienced this in my own consulting firm. We have high expectations for what we can accomplish. At one point the Director of Marketing at Bregman Partners called me to task on this. "Peter, I have 15 top priorities for next week and only two of them are among the top five priorities we established at the beginning of the year. Could you help me prioritize my priorities?" We both had to laugh.

I once heard a consultant speaking to the head of a large division that was undergoing change. The leader had asked the consultant what role he should play in an upcoming meeting with senior executives of the division. The consultant responded, "At three different times during the meeting I want you to slam your hand on the table and say: 'This reorganization is the most important thing we are doing at the company.' I want you to say that at least once in every meeting you attend over the next six months." I learned a lot from that consultant.

**Role Models**: Are *you* living the change you expect others to live? How about other role models in the organization – are they living the change? Sustained action communicates commitment. Most change requires some sacrifice. Are leaders in the organization willing to make that sacrifice too?

Sometimes the change is not pertinent to leaders. Let's expand the definition of role modeling to include avoiding actions that contradict the change and taking actions that support the change. For example, if a leader is not a sales person, then she does not have the opportunity to role model sales behaviors. Instead, the leader can go to the sales floor and watch others sell. She can attend meetings where the new sales skills are being discussed and deliberated. In speeches she can tell stories of seeing those sales behaviors demonstrated. She can reward and praise people who demonstrate those behaviors. On the flip side, a leader should not take actions that contradict the change. She should not praise or reward people who fail to exhibit the behaviors, even if they are successful in other ways. She should not be silent about or absent from the change – in meetings, speeches, and informal conversations. She should not sell, even internally, in the old way.

The most important point I can make about support is that it be persistent. Whatever support you give, keep it up. If you don't, they won't. Maintaining this support over time will ensure that the change will stick.

# 7 STRATEGIES TO CREATING CHANGE!

STRATEGY 1: SHARE THE STORY

STRATEGY 2: KEEP EVERYTHING SIMPLE

STRATEGY 3: GET IT HALF RIGHT

STRATEGY 4: INTEGRATE THE CHANGE

STRATEGY 5: PROVIDE ONGOING SUPPORT

STRATEGY 6: BUILD IN FEEDBACK

STRATEGY 7: USE THE PARTNER SYSTEM

# Strategy 6:
# Build in Feedback

Early in my career, I led a large change effort that was declared a success. But was it? That all depends on who you ask.

The client was a top ten Fortune 500 company and the goal of our work was to improve project management. At the time, projects were consistently late, over budget, and rarely met objectives. Client satisfaction was low.

The leader of this work on the client side was a technologist, as were many of the project managers whose performance he was trying to improve. Because technology was their comfort zone, they looked at the project management problem and saw a technology solution – people were not getting clear and timely information from their current software. So, after a rigorous research and selection process, they chose new project management software to use corporate-wide.

The software was versatile and complex – it included a process for managing projects, communication tools to keep all members of a project team talking with each other, a task management tool so that actions could be delegated over email, and a library of best practices that would be continually updated as projects progressed.

We rolled out the software centrally with a simple goal: within one year, everyone should be using it. Our measurement was equally simple. We measured the percentage of desktops in which the software was installed. The percentage of people who attended the training. The percentage of projects using the new software.

The project was considered a great success because our percentages were high. But were projects now on time, on budget, and meeting their objectives? No. Were clients happier? Of course not.

This program required people to change their behavior. To manage projects in a new way. Our faulty assumption was that new software would result in new behaviors. So the project focused on getting people to use the software. But the problem was not technological, it was behavioral. People weren't talking to each other and they weren't managing customer expectations.

We created a great solution to the wrong problem. And we never realized it because we looked for feedback in the wrong place. We measured our change. Instead we should have measured the impact of our change on customers.

Customer satisfaction is your best predictor of business impact. If your change reduces customer satisfaction, your business will decline. If your change increases customer satisfaction, your business will grow. It really is that simple. When you measure the success of your change, always measure its impact on your customer.

I recently visited an organization and saw that everyone

on the 9th floor had a new 23-inch flat screen monitor on his or her desk. One day, several technologists came to this department with an authorization from "corporate" to upgrade all monitors. Somewhere, on a report about the project called "Install new 23-inch flat screen monitors on every desk in department X," there is a check mark. The project was a success because everyone now had a new monitor. Someone in the change management department of that company is thinking, "If only people were as easy to change as monitors!"

I commented to someone that her screen was beautiful. "Yeah," she said, "it's nice. But I don't really need it. I guess it was just our floor's turn to get them." I asked her if it helped her work faster, better or more comfortably. If her clients were happier. "No," she said, "It doesn't make a difference. I spend most of my time in meetings away from my desk." I asked her what would help her be more effective. "I would love to get a laptop. See, I take notes on paper and I spend a lot of time inputting information into the computer when I get back. That doubles the amount of time I am inaccessible to my clients. If I had a laptop – or even a Palm Pilot with a keyboard – I could take notes during the meetings and then spend more time after meetings with my clients."

Her company spent well over $1,000 to install a new screen on her desk but nobody asked her what she needed. They could have spent half that amount on a Palm Pilot with a keyboard and increased her productivity and her clients' satisfaction immensely. And the impact on her improved morale would have been invaluable. Not only would she have had a tool that was helpful, she would have had the experience of being heard; the opportunity to own a change rather than feel owned by it.

How did her company measure the success of this program? By the number of monitors installed. But why were they installed in the first place? What motivated this investment? Did the investment pay off? These last three questions represent the underlying objectives of the change. They are the only questions that matter.

Traditional change management focuses on the change. Successful change work is focused on the *reason* for the change.

This strategy, Build in Feedback, addresses the highest levels of the Engagement Continuum, reinforcing and strengthening all three attributes of people who change – ownership, capability and persistence.

It is vital that people seek and learn from feedback during change. It is the primary way they will support themselves in the long run and become independent. If I could teach people one skill only, it would be to ask for feedback and then assess how they could change to be more effective. That is the secret to continuous learning. It enables people to grow for a lifetime (as in "give me a fish and I eat for a day, teach me to fish and I eat for a lifetime").

I relentlessly ask for feedback. From colleagues, friends, clients. Even potential clients. Especially potential clients. Recently after a sales call I asked a potential client what I could have done during the meeting to be more effective with her. She was slightly embarrassed at the question. But she answered that I should stick to the point more: give her just the information that she asked for and no more. I thanked her and we set up a second meeting. Can you guess what I did the second time? I was sure to stay to the topic and I won the work.

When I ask for feedback I get valuable information while also communicating my commitment to learning and my desire to partner in an open, communicative way. I don't always change my behavior as a result of the feedback. I take it in as information of how one person sees me. At the very least, I become more aware of my behavior with the person who gave me the feedback. If I agree with the feedback, I can change the way I work with that one person – to create a more productive working relationship. At best, I learn something about myself that may increase my impact with everyone.

At first, I feared that I might lose myself if I kept changing to comply with other people's feedback. I realized, however, that the power to change always remained mine. Feedback is information. It's your choice what to do with it. If you have no desire or intention to do anything with that information (e.g., you have no intention of changing your behavior or improving your relationship with someone, etc.) then don't ask for feedback; it will only result in disappointment. But if you are intent on development and growth, ask away.

Feedback says as much about the person giving the feedback as it does about the person receiving it. Earlier this year, I hired a consultant to help me focus my business and improve my leadership. In preparation for the day, I asked several people (employees, partners, clients, board of directors) to provide me with feedback so that I could discuss it with this consultant. They sent me great responses – some complimentary, others critical, all constructive. The consultant and I spent a day together and he provided me with great help and direction. At the end of the day, I asked him for feedback on our session.

He responded, "I thought the day went more smoothly once you stopped posturing." I asked him what he meant. "When I asked you how you felt about the feedback, you told me you were really excited about it. That it was great to hear the good things and the critical things. C'mon, Peter, nobody *likes* to hear criticism."

I disagreed with him. But he helped me understand a few things. First, while I like feedback of all sorts, many people don't. For that reason, I have to be very careful how and when I give feedback to others. Once I gave some difficult feedback to one of my project managers who was not happy to receive it. I said to her, "You should be happy to receive this feedback. It represents an opportunity for you to improve and become more effective." Oops. Given the intensity of her response, I don't think that was the right thing to say at the time.

I also learned that this consultant viewed feedback differently than me. Perhaps to maintain credibility with him, I should be more reticent in how I respond to his feedback. Perhaps not. But he offered me a clue that when I give *him* feedback, he might not be excited to receive critical information and I should deliver it to him with more sensitivity than I might need if it were delivered to me.

There are several elements to consider when seeking and receiving feedback. The two most important are: Who should ask for feedback? And from whom?

First, who should ask for feedback? *People should measure their own change.* If someone else measures the success of my change, that person is subtly taking responsibility for my change away from me. They own the change. But if I measure my own change, it further reinforces that I own the change. Measuring performance is part of the accountability to change.

Second, from whom should feedback be requested? It is important to measure performance in a way that not only indicates the change is happening and sticking, but also that the change is positively impacting business results. Bottom-line results are, after all, the bottom line. The most important business result for growth and profitability is customer satisfaction. *Ultimately, any change you make should improve your customer relationships.* Therefore, people should get feedback from their customers.

Every employee in an organization has customers. Every change effort should improve customer service in some way. Many employees serve internal customers: their managers, their direct reports, their peers on project teams, members of line units that rely on their work, and others. Some employees serve external customers as well: buyers, suppliers, business partners, clients, and others. Doing a good job means providing quality service to all of one's customers.

There are five benefits to seeking feedback directly from your customers:

First, the people who are responsible for changing are requesting feedback. They are learning while working. This further deepens their engagement and ownership.

Second, asking customers how happy they are with your services makes them happy. It shows that you are committed to improving your service, and that you value their patronage and don't take it for granted.

Third, it communicates to everyone that this organization is serious about change and the way it impacts the bottom line. That message will enhance the effectiveness of change and the accountability of people who are changing.

Fourth, it communicates to people that nothing they do is more important than increasing customer satisfaction. Imagine sending your customer a simple email asking for feedback about behaviors you are striving to demonstrate. And imagine that you sent out the same email once every two months asking whether you have improved since the last time you sent the email. Wouldn't that serve as a reminder to demonstrate the behaviors?

Fifth, it broadcasts that this change will be valued to the extent that people do things differently and that customers are positively impacted.

Often I will hear that asking for feedback is a great idea... in principle. But in reality, I am told, it is not easy to get customers to respond to requests for feedback. I disagree. There are four reasons that changes in customer satisfaction due to organizational change are easy to measure:

First, you can use simple questions or reaction surveys. Now that a person is engaged in a change effort, how does his or her customer perceive their service, their relationship? One simple question could suffice. "What did I do that was helpful to you?" Or "What could I have done that would have been more helpful to you?" Or "What would you like me to do next time?"

Slightly more complicated, but still pretty simple, is a survey. These surveys are easy and inexpensive to create, administer, tabulate, and interpret. They are also a reliable measure of customer satisfaction. It could be as straightforward as an email to a customer that reads:

| To: | ValuedCustomer@email.com |
|---|---|
| Subject: | customer satisfaction |
| Message: | My company is working to improve the way we communicate. I would really appreciate if you could tell me: |
| | Am I listening to you? |
| | Am I answering your questions? |
| | Am I more responsive to your needs? |
| | I will pay close attention to your feedback. Thank you so much for your time and effort in responding. |

Second, reaction sheets for customers get high response rates. Imagine you are a customer who received the simple email shown above. How would you feel? Customers want to give feedback, especially if it is easy to do and they believe it will be taken seriously. Most are delighted to offer an opinion that may help them get better service in the future, or that allows them to express frustration or appreciation.

Third, it is easy to make a valid connection between how someone has changed and how customers feel about that change. By definition, a change program succeeds when it changes people's behaviors *in ways that matter to their customers*. Some examples:

- Customer service and sales reps receive training in active listening. They can ask their customers and prospects whether their concerns are being addressed better than before.
- A manager learns to communicate performance feedback more effectively. She can ask her direct reports whether they understand better how they are doing and what they need to do differently, and whether her feedback motivates or discourages them.
- A change is instituted to prioritize work more carefully in alignment with the organization's new strategy. A person can ask his manager and clients if he meets his deadlines more consistently and produces better quality work.

Fourth, many organizations already ask their customers for feedback. To evaluate the effects of a change, simply ask targeted questions about behaviors relevant to the change, and ask the questions at times that relate to the change (i.e., pre/post/three month follow-up).

Building in feedback focuses on the measurement that people should do themselves. After all, they own the change. They should measure it. In the final strategy, I will discuss the kind of measurement for which the initial leaders of a change must take responsibility and how it can make the difference between a change that sticks and one that slips.

# 7 STRATEGIES TO CREATING CHANGE!

STRATEGY 1: SHARE THE STORY

STRATEGY 2: KEEP EVERYTHING SIMPLE

STRATEGY 3: GET IT HALF RIGHT

STRATEGY 4: INTEGRATE THE CHANGE

STRATEGY 5: PROVIDE ONGOING SUPPORT

STRATEGY 6: BUILD IN FEEDBACK

STRATEGY 7: USE THE PARTNER SYSTEM

# Strategy 7:
# Use The Partner System

I started my career as a trainer. Leading courses for Outward Bound and the National Outdoor Leadership School (NOLS), I took people into the wilderness, sometimes for weeks at a time. Almost invariably, they went through transformational changes. They learned to communicate honestly, take risks, and most important, trust in themselves. Over time, though, people were unable to transfer what they learned in the wilderness to their daily lives.

This is the trainer's dilemma. I might have the best team building training in the world, but if your environment does not support strong teamwork, you will not apply your new skills. You will quickly revert to old habits.

In an effort to solve this dilemma, I joined the Hay Group and later Andersen Consulting (now Accenture) to focus on changing organizational systems. I thought, "If the systems support different behaviors, then people will change their behaviors." I spent five years changing organizations – creating new performance review systems, selection systems, information technology (IT) systems, business process systems – and what I found is that it took people only a few days to circumvent those changes and continue doing things the way they always had.

This is the consultant's dilemma. I might create the best new business process, but if people are not on-board – and I mean really on-board, not simply "OK with it" – then the change won't stick. People won't use it. They will not change.

CHANGE STICKS WHEN BOTH PEOPLE **AND** THEIR ENVIRONMENT CHANGE.

You need to help people change AND shift the environment around them so their changes are truly supported. You don't have to change every aspect of their environment; only what is getting in their way. Changing too much is expensive and creates resistance.

As we have seen, feedback is a crucial part of any change. The Partner System is a method for making precise changes to the environment – not too many, not too few – in support of people who want to change. This strategy is a subtle but strong force, giving people the confidence to persist in their ownership while clearing the obstacles to using their capability, and keeping them at the high end of the Engagement Continuum.

Think of the flowing water of a stream. To keep the stream flowing, we must clear fallen trees and other debris so that they do not divert the water flow. We must also build up the banks so that the water continues to flow in the right direction. That is our job as leaders of change. We clear the obstacles that prevent change and build the structures to move it smoothly forward. People who want to change are the stream; they are the ones moving forward. We do not have to push the water through the riverbed. It will move through on its own as long as we keep the path clear.

The Partner System

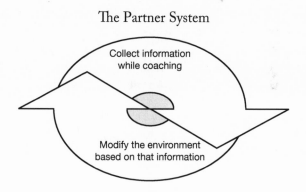

The Partner System is the secret to keeping the path clear. In Strategy 5, Provide Ongoing Support, you learned the QUICC™ Coaching method. In addition to providing ongoing support, coaching provides timely organizational intelligence throughout the change. When people are coached, they offer their coaches valuable information about themselves and their organization. What trends are arising? What obstacles are people facing? What objections are they offering? What successes are they realizing? What organizational structures are getting in their way? What organizational issues are helping or hindering the success of change?

This information contains precise direction regarding which elements of the environment need to be modified to support others. While maintaining the confidentiality of each individual, coaches share general information about trends and issues. After a series of coaching sessions, coaches can guide organizational leaders to develop the organization (e.g., culture, processes, roles, etc.) and remove obstacles to better position their people for success.

As we coached people in the organization in which we were improving the rates of performance reviews, we uncovered several issues.

First, we noticed a major gap in communication skills. In many cases, even people who had written performance reviews in the past never actually spoke about the reviews with their employees. Also, communication was the number one performance issue that managers needed to address with their employees; many employees were technical experts who were ineffective at speaking with or presenting to clients.

Second, the performance review forms themselves were complicated and cumbersome. Managers were as new to the competency-based forms as the employees were. The complexity of the forms combined with their lack of communication skills created fear that they would look unskilled in front of their employees.

Third, even in the newly shortened just-in-time trainings, managers were in the same classes as their employees and felt too vulnerable to ask questions that might expose their inexperience.

Fourth, there were several competing business initiatives that leaders declared high priority. This sent mixed messages to reviewers.

Fifth, the language of the competencies was confusing to many people.

We also heard about things that were helpful to them. The shortened training was focused and provided useful information. The coaching made a big difference; people were delighted that they could get specific support in planning their conversations. Setting an appointment with their coach created intermediate deadlines that reduced their procrastination.

These were hands-on issues that we could not have discovered until we put the theory of the change into action. It is hard to know where people will be overwhelmed, where they will be confused, where the greatest needs are, and what's enabling them.

The traditional approach is to do a huge amount of up-front research, focus groups, surveys, and interviews, followed by a pilot, culminating in a program that will anticipate and address these issues up front. Of course, similar issues pop up in those changes too. The difference is that the leaders of those changes have spent more time and money designing up front and are therefore reluctant to make the changes necessary for the program to succeed.

Psychologically, this traditional approach minimizes risk and blame. If I do an enormous amount of work to design and prepare for a change, then I am beyond reproach. If the change does not work, or does not stick, it is not for lack of effort or preparation. It is not my fault. If, however, I have only prepared half-way and leave the rest to its eventual unfolding and inevitable course corrections, I take on a higher perceived risk. The actual risk is no greater. But it is easier to blame me for not having done enough work in preparing for the change. Thankfully, there is a way out of this dilemma.

Do the preparation. But don't over-prepare the change, its content, or the process for using the content (who needs to do what, when). Instead, prepare for the process of managing the change itself. Plan for the inevitable shifts you will make to ensure the change is alive and moving with people's needs. Plan ways to collect information during the change. Plan your methods for modifying the change once it leaves the design table and lands in the hearts and minds and hands of the people who are changing.

The Partner System is an important ingredient of that planning. When people complain about the obstacles, they can use the QUICC™ Coaching process to transform their complaints into action. They don't simply collect the trend and obstacle information; they help people work through it so it does not paralyze them or the change.

In our performance review client, coaches helped people gain the communication skills and confidence they needed to have difficult conversations. They planned the conversations together in the coaching session. They answered questions that managers felt too vulnerable to ask in class. They helped managers understand the competencies and apply them to specific employee situations. They planned with managers to identify priorities around various other initiatives to ensure that this one did not fall through the cracks. Coaches and managers circumvented problems together on a case-by-case basis.

At the same time, coaches could truthfully tell managers and employees that the obstacles raised would be brought to management attention. That they could find temporary ways to work around those obstacles knowing that more permanent solutions would be sought. They were not left alone to fend for themselves. That offered tremendous motivation to people who would otherwise have felt powerless.

Coaches fed this trend information to the business unit subcommittees so they could further revise the program. We did not make critical decisions. They did. In many cases, the people who raised the obstacles were on the subcommittees and could make the changes themselves. This further deepened their engagement and ownership, continuously strengthening the change.

At the request of the people who were choosing to change, we simplified the competencies and the performance review forms. We created several new JETS™ trainings followed by coaching to improve communication and presentation skills. We separated managers and employees for all performance review JETS™ trainings. We worked with senior business leaders to prioritize the various initiatives; sometimes we changed the performance review schedule to accommodate those priorities, sometimes we lowered the priorities of the competing initiatives, sometimes we simply had to work out ways to get it all done at the same time. We continued using the JETS™ training and the QUICC™ coaching since these were helpful to people.

The Partner System gave us an incredible amount of valuable information about which structures needed to change and which didn't. We minimized expensive organizational change by focusing solely on the changes that would have the biggest impact.

ONLY CHANGE THE THINGS THAT ARE IN THE WAY.

We didn't redesign their compensation structure. We didn't create an all-encompassing training and development curriculum. We didn't change the computer-based performance review system. We didn't change the process of selecting reviewers. We didn't change the number of competencies or their behaviorally based anchors. These were all things we considered changing before the program was launched, but we chose to wait and see if they were obstacles. They were not, and we saved a lot of money and effort by leaving them intact.

This process is instrumental in avoiding resistance. Who is telling you what to change? The very people who would have resisted if those changes were imposed on them. So resistance is transformed into request. Resistors are transformed into leaders. And people will help make those changes because they own them, because they suggested them in the first place. When you listen to them and help them change their obstacles, they will do everything in their power to make the change successful. To make the organization succeed.

The Partner System also measures the success of the change process. It provides clear information to support the other six change strategies. Through the Partner System you will discover:

1.  Is the story clear and compelling?
2.  Are the methods simple enough?
3.  Do people own the change? Do they have the right amount of input into the strategy?
4.  Is the change smoothly integrated with their work?
5.  Do they have enough support? Is it the right support?
6.  Are the right people getting the right feedback from the right people?

The Partner System is effective because, like the other six strategies, it gives people control over their change. They have the information and the power to modify the change "real time." They have intense flexibility supported by real data that generates a never-ending learning loop: create a change as needed by the organization. Measure the change through the Partner System. Modify the change as needed by people who are making the choice to change. Measure the modification of the change through the Partner System. Change the modification of the change as needed by people who are changing. And so on.

Together, these strategies enable people to maintain the ownership, capability, and persistence to ensure that their change sticks without ever getting stuck.

# Conclusion

Much of this book has focused on letting go of, or sharing, control; supporting others' interest in controlling their own contributions to change. All this aside, we must remember that we each have full control over ourselves, our actions, and our own behaviors in the context of change. What each of us does, says, thinks and feels has the potential to significantly impact change. I want to tell you three inspiring and true stories of remarkable, instantaneous change.

## Gandhi

Gandhi was a man who knew something about large-scale change. Gandhi's grandson Arun tells how Gandhi would receive visitors seeking advice, blessing, or other spiritual aid. Indian villagers would travel for hundreds of miles for a brief audience with the Mahatma. One pair of such visitors was a woman and her young son, a diabetic. When her turn in line came, she implored Gandhi to tell her son to stop eating sugar. "Please, Mahatma, he doesn't listen to me. He'll listen to you. Tell him that sugar will kill him."

Gandhi looked at the woman and the boy and said, "Come back in three weeks." He indicated that the next supplicant should approach. The woman was mortified. To be dismissed thus by the great man! Nevertheless, she did as she was told. She and her son returned to their village, and three weeks later, at great effort and expense, they returned to wait on the long line once again. This time, when their turn came, before she could remind Gandhi of their previous encounter, he looked at the boy with intense fierceness and determination and roared, "Don't eat sugar!" The boy was shocked and transformed in that instance. He would never touch sugar again. The mother, exhausted from her two trips, demanded an explanation from Gandhi. Why couldn't he have done that three weeks ago and saved them a second trip? "Madam," he explained respectfully, "Three weeks ago, I was still eating sugar."

### Ariyaratne

The second story moves us a bit south, to the island state of Sri Lanka. The founder and leader of a rural renewal and health and education movement, A.T. Ariyaratne, had made many powerful enemies among the ruling class who saw his populist movement as a threat to their position. Ari, as he is known, was once scheduled to speak in a Hindu temple in the capital city of Colombo. He was tipped off the day before that a political leader had hired a hit man, a ruthless crime boss, to assassinate him at this event. Ari knocked on the hit man's door that evening, explained who he was, and requested that the assassination be carried out there and then, to prevent the temple from being desecrated with his blood. The hit man not only refused to kill him, but in that instance gave up his life of crime and became Ari's devoted follower.

## Weisser

The third story brings us to Nebraska in 1991. A cantor, Michael Weisser, was newly installed in a small Reform Jewish congregation in Lincoln when he and his family began receiving threatening letters and phone calls from the Grand Dragon of the Nebraska KKK. The klansman, a hateful man named Larry Trapp, was already responsible for provoking attacks on the persons and property of prominent African-American members of the community. He was only able to provoke because he had lost his legs and his eyesight to diabetes. Fearful and angry, Weisser nevertheless held fast to his belief that love was stronger than hate. He began leaving messages on Trapp's answering machine, after enduring the ten-minute diatribes that were the outgoing messages. He asked questions: "Larry, what will you say to God when you die? ... Larry, how does it feel to carry around so much hate? ... Larry, did you know that the Third Reich killed cripples first? Why do you love Hitler so much?"

Then one day, while Weisser was leaving a message, Trapp picked up the phone. "Who the hell are you? What do you want?" Weisser was surprised, but prepared by his faith. He answered, "Larry, I saw you on TV and I know you're in a wheelchair. I thought maybe I could help take you shopping for groceries." The edge vanished from Trapp's voice. "No, that's OK. I'm OK. Thanks." Weisser sensed that the resistance was crumbling, and said that he and his wife were coming over anyway. They informed the police what they were doing, just in case, but it wasn't necessary. No sooner had Trapp opened the door than he began sobbing, begging them to forgive him, begging them to help him change. Trapp later explained, "When I heard his voice I knew there was something in the world better than the hate I was living. I knew I needed that thing before I died."

Within a couple of days, Trapp had resigned from the Klan, called people he had tormented and begged their forgiveness, and burned decades of collected white supremacist materials. His change was real and permanent.

What do these three people show us about who we should be as people who lead change? I want to highlight three characteristics.

The first is **integrity**. Gandhi waited until he was no longer eating sugar before he told the child not to eat sugar. He did not ask someone to do something that he himself would not do. He lived the change before asking anyone else to live the change. And he was direct, open, and honest in his communication. He admitted to having eaten sugar before and having to stop before he could issue the command. And he issued the command simply and straightforwardly. With presence, but without going into a long selling job about why it was in the child's best interest to stop eating sugar. He stopped the sugar himself, and then simply stated, *Stop eating sugar*. Think about the changes that you are leading. Are you living them yourself? Are you doing what you are asking others to do? What do you really feel and think about the change? What are you saying about the change? Are they the same? Test your integrity with someone you really trust. Practice telling them the complete truth about how you feel. What would it take for you to be public about your feelings and to ensure that you were in line with your beliefs?

The second is **vulnerability**. Ariyaratne exposed himself to his own assassin. He gave ultimate control to his enemy. Maybe he was just lucky. But there is also power in being vulnerable. Allowing yourself to be open to the risk of being exposed. So maybe you aren't an expert. Or maybe you are and you are willing to put that expertise aside to learn from others. Think about what you are afraid of. When you go into a meeting, a training room, a focus group, consider: what are you protecting? Why are you defensive? What could you say (or not say), do (or not do) that would allow others to move forward – even though it might make you feel less secure, less smart, less experienced? Try to clarify your fears. Try to name what you are protecting. It will help you get over it. Remember: it is very rare for people to have to deal with actual assassination attempts.

The third is **caring**. Weisser had a deep faith in people and a powerful caring for others. Do you care about others? Do you truly care about their lives, their experience at the company, their opinions, their fears, their vulnerability? That is the key to listening to them, to wanting them to create their own changes, to helping them take control. Caring means re-membering why organizations exist in the first place: to make the world a better place, to enable people to achieve collectively and collaboratively what they cannot achieve individually.

Maintain the principles of this book, use its strategies, and live your change with integrity, vulnerability, and caring. Your change will succeed.

Made in the USA